SWANSEA
IN 100 DATES

GEOFF BROOKES

T0346940

The
History
Press

To Liz, my wife,
who brought me to Swansea in the first place.

First published 2015

The History Press
The Mill, Brimscombe Port
Stroud, Gloucestershire, GL5 2QG
www.thehistorypress.co.uk

© Geoff Brookes, 2015

The right of Geoff Brookes to be identified as the Author
of this work has been asserted in accordance with the
Copyright, Designs and Patents Act 1988.

British Library Cataloguing in Publication Data.
A catalogue record for this book is available from the British Library.

ISBN 978 0 7524 9909 3

Typesetting and origination by The History Press
Printed in Great Britain

Contents

About the Author

Geoff Brookes is a writer with a long-standing interest in Welsh history. A prolific author of local history titles, he has written *Bloody Welsh History: Swansea*, *Swansea Then & Now*, *Swansea Murders* and *Welsh History: Strange but True* for The History Press. He lives in Swansea.

www.geoffbrookes.co.uk

Introduction

This is, on reflection, a random collection of events, selected from the strange and often untold history of Swansea. The book has a simple concept – 100 dates – and the things that happened on them. There are so many other things that could have been included but didn't make it. Some of the famous people who were born in Swansea don't get a mention. But what I hope is that the book gives an impression of our past through the news items that I have selected.

Let's be honest, Swansea has never really been at the heart of things. It has never been a place where big decisions have shaped the world's future; but this is its charm. If you look closely at its story, a window will open into the past through which you can see exactly how life was led, how the emotions and priorities that still drive us today were played out in different times. You will meet violence and abject poverty, exploitation and shattered dreams. And you will realise that the people in these brief extracts were no different from us. Just as we do, they lived their lives in an untidy, unplanned way. But this is how the future has always been shaped; always accidentally and always by ordinary people.

Murder, war, industrial accidents, family tragedy, stupidity – all these play their own part in our story. In this book you will meet the real people of Swansea: our ancestors, those who we are ashamed of, and our heroes too. There were plenty of those. It is a town – or city – that has bred resilience and fortitude. It has always been a place divided too, between west and east, between wealth and poverty, between those with the money and those who actually created it – and often suffered for it. This is Swansea, where men fell into vats of molten metal whilst their employers lived away from the poisonous smoke and the filth, developed photography and played around in boats.

The events that appear in this book are those that shaped our city. They have been researched entirely from contemporary sources and I must thank all those unknown and unacknowledged journalists who recorded all these stories in the first place. Without their work, this book would have been impossible. I would also like to extend my admiration and gratitude to the journalists of today, who record the things that we do. And then perhaps one day our own idiocies will be published for the wonder of our great-great grandchildren, who will shake their heads at all the stupid things we have done.

SWANSEA
IN 100 DATES

1 January

1136

The Battle of Garngoch, also known as the Battle of Llwchwr or the Battle of Penllergaer, took place on this day. It remains one of the most significant battles in Welsh history. A Norman force, marching out of Gower to confront what they thought was a Welsh raiding party, found themselves surrounded by a properly organised army. Trapped in mud, the Normans were slaughtered. According to the historian William Camden, the Welsh 'slew divers men of quality and good account'. At least 516 were said to have been killed. This defeat encouraged Welsh insurrection for the next 150 years.

1910

'The Christmas-tide festivities were never more freely and more whole-heartedly indulged in at Swansea than this year, thanks to the extraordinary industrial prosperity which has prevailed throughout the year, all classes thus having been provided with the wherewithal in exceptional abundance.' (*The Cardiff Times*)

1916

The SS *Dunvegan* ran aground in heavy seas at Pennard after suffering from engine failure. The Port Eynon lifeboat – the *Janet* – was launched, although the crew of the *Dunvegan* were saved by land-based rescuers. Sadly the *Janet* was swamped and three members of the crew were lost in what became known as 'the Port Eynon Lifeboat Disaster'. The men are remembered on an impressive memorial in Port Eynon churchyard.

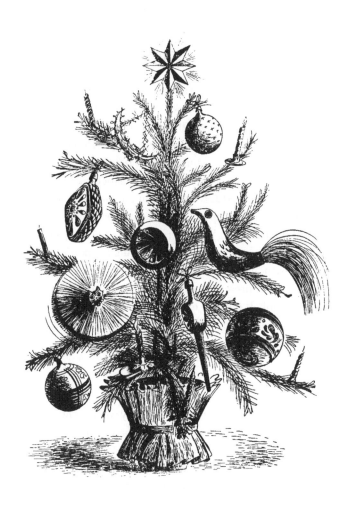

9 January

1918

The government developed a scheme to raise money for the war effort through the Tank Bank. Tanks toured the country and the public were invited see the new machines and to invest in War Saving Certificates. These were sold at 15*s* 6*d* and would be returned in five years' time as £1 – representing 5.4 per cent tax-free interest. Investors were described as 'Fifteen and Sixers'. A tank called *Egbert* arrived in the town on this date and Swansea was caught up in 'Tank Bank Fever'. *Egbert* was placed in Guildhall Square, Wind Street having been rejected since it might lead to traffic disruption. To fuel the patriotic fervour Mrs O'Brien, mother of Sergeant Pat O'Brien of the Swansea Battalion, was presented with his posthumous Military Cross from the tank. It became extremely competitive, with Swansea desperate to raise more money through *Egbert* that Llanelli could raise through its tank, *Julian*.

1941

'We were going to have supper when Jerry was passing over. Had to leave supper as shooting was very bad. Just as I'm writing a plane has passed over but we have not had a warning so far. We still go to bed with clothes on.' (From the diary of Hannah Rees, Brynhyfryd. Used with the permission of her grand-daughter Eileen Bristow.)

12 January

1810

This is the birthday of the local scientist John Dillwyn Llewelyn (1810–1882). He was a botanist and photographic pioneer who indulged his interests on his estate at Penllergare. Here he created a private orchid house and kept a boat powered by an electric motor on his lake. He also had his own observatory. The house, meanwhile, was heated by recycling waste steam. In 1844 he was involved in experiments in underwater telegraphy, using submerged wires in Swansea to enable a boat to communicate with the Mumbles lighthouse. But it is his pioneering photographic work for which he is best remembered.

Most of his pictures were taken on the estate and he developed the Oxymel process, using honey and vinegar to preserve images, making it easier to take pictures in outdoor settings.

1906

The *Cambrian News* reported that 'the pleasures of the table are not for the singer' in a story about the singer Adelina Patti. When she was due to sing she ate beef and potatoes, followed by baked apples in the late afternoon. The beef was intended to give force to the voice and apples smoothness. 'After dinner the prima donna fasts until she sings', only taking between the acts of the opera 'homeopathic doses of phosphorus and capsicum'.

1792

Margaret Geary from Swansea was in service with Paul Chadwick in Sloane Street, Knightsbridge. She was indicted at the Old Bailey on this day for stealing a £50 note from Chadwick's study. She claimed that she had been cleaning the study and found a piece of paper on the floor. Being unable to read or write, and therefore unaware it was a banknote, she put it in her pocket. Margaret was found guilty of theft and sentenced to death.

1893

The *Cambrian News* reported:

> For unlawfully and maliciously breaking three panes of glass at the Wassail Inn, and also with doing damage to three enamelled letters, glass and gold, two trademarks, and one plate glass in frame, with name of house embossed in gold, the property of Ellen Morgan, the landlady, Annie Taylor, of ill-repute, was sent to prison for three calendar months with hard labour. The damage done amounted to £5 19s and was the result of a very violent temper.

Taylor, it appears, was refused drink at the public house, 'whereupon she went outside and pelted the windows with stones'.

1916

Private W.J. Sandywell, serving with the Swansea Battalion, died in the trenches when he was accidentally shot by a colleague. He was a married man with five children.

16 January

1857

The *Pembrokeshire Herald* reported the case of a man called Duggan, who was sentenced to transportation for life for the burglary of Mr Moses, a jeweller in Swansea. In Cardiff Gaol he attempted to murder one of the warders by striking him on the head with a large piece of firewood. He then tried to strangle himself by tying one end of his neckerchief to the window bars, but was rescued. Soon it was noticed that Duggan's eyes were deteriorating, 'as if they had been scratched'. In one of his pockets they found a very small piece of glass, 'with which he had scratched the pupils of the eyes to such an extent as to make it doubtful whether the sight will ever be perfectly restored'. He explained his actions by saying he had no desire to be sent out of the country.

1962

The feature film *Only Two Can Play* was released. It starred Peter Sellers and Mai Zetterling and is set in the fictional town of Aberdarcy. Based on the novel *That Uncertain Feeling* by Kingsley Amis, it was filmed on location in Swansea and became the first cinema release to receive an X-certificate rating.

1823

William Buckland climbed down into Goat's Hole at Paviland in Gower to find the skeleton known as 'The Red Lady of Paviland'. Whilst it was not the remains of a lady, it was the first human fossil ever found. It was a ceremonial Palaeolithic burial dating from about 27,000 BC.

1939

Sometime during the early hours of the morning, Ruth Webber died at No. 38 Trafalgar Terrace. She was found in bed with her legs and the lower part of her torso burnt away.

She had met Allan Maclean, a Scottish seaman. They had returned to her room drunk and had begun arguing. Maclean hit her and threw her on the bed, covering her with blankets he grabbed from the floor, inadvertently picking up an oil lamp too. This ignited the bedding, which smouldered all night. Ruth, drunk and beaten, never woke up. Maclean was found guilty of manslaughter and sent to prison for five years.

2008

The BBC reported that scientists had posted jellyfish spotters on Irish Sea ferries as part of their research into a species known as 'mauve stingers'. It was feared that they could swarm along the Welsh coastline, so a marine biologist at Swansea University was given £50,000 to find out how many there were between Wales and Ireland. Consequently, spotters stood on deck, staring at the sea and counting jellyfish.

22 January

1879

Private David Jenkins, who claimed that he fought at the Battle of Rorke's Drift, which took place on this day, was presented to King Edward VII on his visit to Swansea in 1904. It was discovered that he had been omitted from the Roll of Honour of those who had fought there. Following extensive research by his descendants, he was reinstated in 2013. However, there are still those who question his presence during the engagement. David Jenkins died in 1912 and is buried in Cwmgelli Cemetery, Treboeth.

1949

The body of Ernest Melville, a 38-year-old 'chain man' working for Swansea Corporation in the Borough Engineer's department, was found by two girls playing hide and seek. He had been beaten to death with a stone on a bombsite next to Dyfatty Park on Croft Street. Melville lived with his parents on Watkin Street and had that night been playing the piano in the Full Moon public house. Despite extensive enquiries, including the questioning of every sailor known to have been in Swansea that night, the murder has never been solved. Melville's homosexual lifestyle was regarded as the key element in his death. Neither the tall man in a trench coat in the Palace Bar, nor the two sailors seen opposite the station that the police were anxious to question, were ever traced.

27 January

1883

During a severe storm, eighteen men were lost at Port Eynon when the *Agnes Jack* was wrecked, most of them dashed to death on the rocks. In another incident the German vessel, *Admiral-Prinz Adalbert*, was driven on to the rocks below the Mumbles lighthouse. The lifeboat was launched and managed to get a line aboard. Two men were recovered but the lifeboat was swamped and the crew made for the shore. Four of them, with one previously rescued sailor, were drowned. Two sisters, Jessie and Margaret Ace, daughters of the lighthouse keeper, waded into the sea to save two survivors by throwing out their shawls and dragging the men ashore. They were celebrated in the narrative poem 'The Women of Mumbles Head', written by Clement Scott and frequently performed in music halls. All crewmembers that remained on board the *Adalbert* survived, and the Ace sisters were awarded medals by the German government.

There was also a fire in Mr Williams' shop in Lower Oxford Street, where he stocked Royal Daylight Petroleum Oil. He and his wife escaped but their two sons died when the house was destroyed, along with the roofs of adjoining properties. Sadly, the water pressure from the hydrants was insufficient. The water came from Felindre reservoir and in the lower parts of Swansea, the water was turned off at night to maintain pressure for the higher districts.

28 January

1804

The first edition of the *Cambrian News*, Swansea's very own newspaper and unrivalled resource for local historians, was published from offices on Wind Street on Saturday, 28 January 1804. It was the first English-language newspaper published in Wales and ran for 126 years, appearing weekly. The final edition, No. 6,204, was printed on Friday, 14 March 1930, after which it was merged with the *Herald of Wales*.

1843

Owing to a shortage of local foxes, three were brought in sacks from London, to 'be turned out before the foxhounds'. They were kept in the stables of the Castle Hotel. One of the foxes, however, escaped during the night through the window, so a huntsman took two hounds to find him. 'They struck on his trail' near Fynonne and chased the fox for 12 miles, until he was cornered by the dogs in Sketty. 'The huntsman, who was on foot, and within 200 yards, failed to come up in time to save the poor fox for another day's sport.' The following day another of the foxes was released near Fairwood Lodge, 'before a large field of sportsmen, well mounted'. They gave him half an hour's start. 'He went off in good style, and was killed in Clyne Wood.' The third fox was taken out to the common, but when the flour sack was opened, it was discovered that the fox had suffocated.

6 February

1830

'Another instance of the dangerous and reprehensible practice of leaving charged fire-arms within reach of boys occurred last week at Mile End. A child, eighteen months old, having been left in a small chair during the momentary absence of the mother, her brother, a lad about 16 years entered, and observing the gun, laid hold of it to amuse himself, and while examining the piece, it went off, and killed the poor infant on the spot.' (*Cambrian News*)

1846

Following heavy rain, houses in the area around Wellington Road and the lower parts of the town were flooded. One house was occupied by John Morgan, surveyor, who found a 5ft-long conger eel in his living room. (*Cambrian News*)

1888

David Davies, a 25-year-old seaman, slashed his wife Mary Jane to death with a razor at their home in Hall Street, Waun Wen. He admitted the murder and also acknowledged hearing voices. He was detained in Broadmoor Hospital, being released in 1898 but quickly readmitted. He died in Broadmoor in 1912.

8 February

1915

Willie Rees, aged 9, from Trewyddfa Road, drowned in the Morriston Canal on his way to the Landore Cinema. He was walking on the edge of the canal, slipped and fell into the water 'which at that particular spot is about 7ft. deep. A friend attempted to clutch Willie, but only managed to grasp his cap. The body was in the water for an hour before it was picked up by a man named Clarke. Much sympathy is felt for the bereaved family, who are highly respected in the district.' (*Cambrian Daily Leader*)

1963

Mr Saunders of Llangyfelach handed the police a brown paper bag that he had found in his garden. It contained a blue petticoat, one black bra, three pairs of panties (two black and one mauve) and three brown stockings. The items were never claimed. (*Swansea Police Found Property Log Book*, 1963)

2010

The cathedral in Santiago, Chile, was destroyed in a fire in December 1863, when almost 3,000 people were killed. The cathedral bells were sent to Swansea to be melted down but were rescued and installed in All Saints church in Mumbles. Sadly, due to structural issues, the church bells were not rung for fifty years. On this day, it was agreed to return them to Chile to be reinstalled in time for the 150th anniversary of the disaster.

10 February

1810

John Lucas died after receiving a blow from machinery in a mill at Reynoldston. A ramrod he held in his hand was driven into his eye, and fractured his skull. (*Cambrian News*)

1840

The vault of Sir Mathew Cradock (1468–1531) in St Anne's chapel in St Mary's church was opened by the historically curious. Cradock had been steward of Gower in 1491 and 1497. Inside there were five coffins, but no inscriptions were visible. It was assumed that the oldest coffin was his.

1929

Kate Jackson was found beaten around the head outside her home in Limeslade. She died in hospital six days later. She had previously claimed to be the reclusive novelist Ethel Dell and had appeared in court as 'Madame X' during the trial of William Harrison. He was the secretary of the National Association of Coopers and had been embezzling funds from the union to give to Kate, who had claimed to be carrying his child and needed a termination. She later asserted to have received death threats from union members angry about the disappearance of their money. But little of what Kate said was true. She was an ex-prostitute, probably murdered by her husband Thomas Jackson, who bludgeoned her with a tyre lever. He was accused of her murder and arrested, but was found not guilty in court and released.

19 February

1903

The celebrated actor Henry Irving and his 'Lyceum Company' appeared at the Swansea Grand Theatre. It was a sell-out, establishing a record for receipts. The audience were treated to a performance of a drama called *Waterloo* followed by *The Bells*, in which Irvine played his most famous role as Mathias.

1941

Although Swansea was bombed during the Second World War on forty occasions, the most serious raids were those that started on this day and became known as 'The Three Day Blitz'. The records show that 230 people died, while 400 were injured. Approximately 41 acres of the town centre were destroyed.

Each attack began with the dropping of parachute flares, and then incendiary bombs followed by high explosives. Strangely, not enough bombs were dropped for it to be officially classified as either a blitz or indeed a 'major attack'. Nonetheless, 857 buildings were destroyed, 11,000 were damaged and forty-eight major sewers and forty-seven gas mains were severed. On this night, sixty-one German aircraft from northern France were involved in a 3½-hour attack. The first incident attended by the Auxiliary Fire Service was at No. 91 Rhondda Street at 8.05 p.m. In the worst single incident of the Three Nights, forty-six people were killed and forty-four injured when six bombs fell on Teilo Crescent, Mayhill on 20 February.

23 February

1867

Jacob Rees was a worker at Lambert's Copper Works in Port Tennant. As he opened the furnace, he fell from the plank on which he was standing into the pit below. It was filled with molten copper and he was instantly burnt to death. He left a wife and three children.

1941

The *Wartime Diary of Laurie Latchford, Air-Raid Warden*, records:

Someone said that 240 people were trapped under the Wesley Chapel. Although I knew this area intimately, I found it impossible to identify the shops which had stood there … The front wall of the Chapel, the large notice board giving details of divine services and side walls had survived. By one side wall was an emergency exit from the crypt. I went down a few steps. My feelings were not nice. I shone my torch. Still steaming water was dripping from the buckled ceiling. My torch showed water below, and at the far end of the crypt, a heat-whitened tin hat. I went down. I have never made such an effort of will before … I went down another three steps and thrust my walking stick into the water. It was only about six inches deep! There was certainly no one there, dead or alive.

(West Glamorgan Archive Service)

28 February

1890

The *Cambrian News* remarked on the state of Swansea's streets:

> Frightened and half-wild cattle are driven through the streets of Swansea without sufficient cow-herds to manage them; and gangs of school boys play football as they go to and from school; and carts and traps and carriages are constantly driven through our thoroughfares in such a careless manner and at such high speed as to cause disquietude and discomfort, and even seriously to imperil the limbs and lives of the townsfolk.

1948

Evan Harris from Tycoch, a 73-year-old nightwatchman in the docks, was found dead in shallow water at the stern of the ship *Brecon Castle* in the Consolidated Fisheries dry dock. He was a widower who appears to have been known as a moneylender. Harris had been beaten around the head with a piece of wood in a shed and then dragged to the dockside and thrown in where he had drowned in 1ft of water. There were severe cuts to his face and his skull was broken in many places.

The police spent a long time looking for a particular suspect who had been seen in St Thomas and who had lost most of the middle finger of his left hand. Despite appeals for information broadcast in local cinemas, the police were unable to make progress with their enquiries. No one has ever been charged with his murder.

29 February

1896

The *South Wales Daily Post* reported that the Swansea Empire had booked a new novelty act who had caused a big sensation in Bristol. This was Zanetto, who would catch a turnip or an orange thrown from the auditorium on the prongs of a fork held in his mouth. Previously in Bristol he had drawn an audience in excess of 5,000, who watched him catch turnips – dropped from the Clifton Suspension Bridge – on a two-pronged fork. Five turnips were dropped before he succeeded because, he said, they kept being caught by the wind.

1964

Swansea Town played Liverpool at Anfield in the sixth round of the FA Cup, which Swansea won 2–1. Swansea then lost to Preston North End in the semi-final, also by a score of 2–1.

2004

In a protest against the introduction of higher tuition fees, a student put the entire Swansea University Campus up for sale on the auction site eBay. By this stage, with ten days left, the bidding had reached £54.89, perhaps reflecting the fact that the property came complete with 13,000 students. The BBC reported that the vice chancellor said he had been encouraging 'entrepreneurial thinking', but was 'surprised that it had gone this far'.

1 March

1738

We hear from Swansey in Glamorganshire that last week Mr James Dalton, Waiter and Searcher at Penclawdd within the Port of Swansey made a seizure of 1700 weight of tea, several anchors of Brandy and Rum and two boxes of rich chints, callicoes, persians and other things, the whole being the greatest seizure that ever was made in that country.

(*The Derby Mercury*)

1880

William Davies, captain of the *Standard Bearer*, appeared at the Old Bailey accused of murder. The ship had left Swansea for South America in March 1879 and, during the outward voyage, his behaviour had been so unpredictable that the crew were apprehensive about their return. The British Consul in Talcahano, Chile, refused to hear their complaints and ordered them to sail. On Christmas Day Davies, who was drinking heavily and was hearing voices, shot and killed the steward, William Price, and locked himself in his cabin. Davies was found not guilty of murder on the grounds of insanity and detained 'until Her Majesty's pleasure be known'.

1997

Councillors in Swansea agreed to lift an eighteen-year ban on screenings of the film *The Life of Brian*. It had originally been condemned as blasphemous and councillors refused the film a licence; one councillor described it as 'unmitigated filth'. The ban was finally removed in order to allow a showing to raise funds for Comic Relief.

4 March

1881

William Williams, a 'burly rosy-cheeked individual', summoned his wife Elizabeth Williams for assaulting him and threatening his life. The court found it hard to take the case seriously and William was mocked by Mr Woodward for the defence as a 'big baby'. Nevertheless, he was frightened of Elizabeth. She had threatened him when he came in from feeding his horse, telling him that if he entered the house she would 'rip him with a knife', then in her hand. He backed away and she threw stones at him, hurting his leg. He had to sleep in the stable.

The charge of assault was dismissed but Elizabeth was bound over in the sum of £10 to keep the peace for a month.

1904

David and Hannah Jenkins of Tontine Street were summoned for neglecting their children, who were described by the *Cambrian News* as 'verminous': the children lived in a house 'frequented by thieves'; their eldest son was himself a convicted thief and the prisoners themselves were in and out of prison, and the girls slept in the same room as 'prostitutes and men who were engaged in immoral acts'. David was sentenced to prison for three months and Hannah for two. She went to the cells singing and shouting obscenities.

7 March

1876

Edgar Evans was born in Rhossili and died on Captain Scott's Antarctic expedition in 1912. He attended St Helen's Boys School and after enlisting in the Royal Navy in 1891, was invited to join Scott's first expedition on the *Discovery* in 1901. He nearly didn't make the second expedition in *Terra Nova* when, extremely drunk, he fell into the harbour in New Zealand when boarding and had to be rescued. On the return journey from the Pole, Evans had severe frostbite to fingers, nose and cheeks and suffered a serious head injury when he fell into a crevasse. His widow and mother of their three children, Lois, installed a plaque in remembrance in the church in Rhossili.

1978

The skull of Emanuel Swedenborg, the Swedish philosopher, spent some years in Swansea. He died in London in 1772 and when placed in a coffin in a Swedish Seaman's church, the skull was removed. It eventually turned up in Swansea in the possession of a doctor, whose father had bought it in a junk shop in London, where it had been helpfully labelled as 'The Genuine Skull of Swedenborg'. On 7 March 1978 it was auctioned at Sotheby's, where it was purchased by the Royal Academy of Science in Stockholm and reunited with the rest of the skeleton in Uppsala.

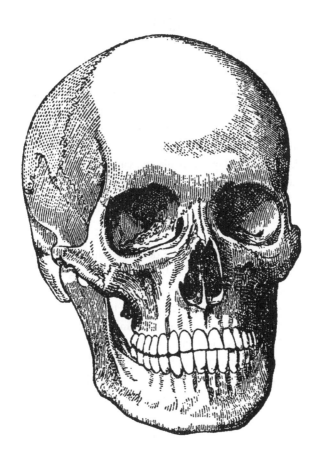

8 March

1834

Rosser Mort and John Jones appeared in court after breaking into two houses in Foxhole. They went on the run and were eventually detained after a vicious struggle in Greenhill. They were sentenced to death but the sentences were commuted to transportation for life. Mort left on the *George the Third* for Tasmania (then known as Van Diemen's Land) in December with another 219 convicts. The ship hit rocks off the coast of Tasmania and sank; 129 convicts trapped in the hold, including Rosser Mort, were drowned.

1901

The *Cambrian News* reported the death of John Holbein Rosser, aged 19, the son of a livery stables owner of Dysgwylfa House in Sketty. He had completed his university course and had been articled to a firm of mining engineers. He had gone to the doctor suffering from a 'catarrhal headache' and 'Dr Dan' Evans had prescribed him a medicinal 'draught'. Unfortunately it was wrongly labelled: 'Dr Dan' had stuck a label on the wrong bottle and instead gave him 'pure carbolic acid'. 'John Rosser passed away clinging to his mother.' The coroner's verdict was 'death by misadventure'.

1907

Thomas Rees was badly injured in a roof-fall at the Commercial Colliery in Killay and was carried home in an ambulance. On arrival he found that his wife had left him, taking their 2-month-old baby and leaving him with their other four children, all under 6 years old.

10 March

2013

Princess Lilian of Sweden, Duchess of Halland, died on this day in Stockholm aged 97. She had been born in Swansea as Lillian May Davies in 1915. Her parents were market traders and lived on Garden Street, now buried beneath the Quadrant. She left her job in a laundry and went to London where, looking a little like Marlene Dietrich, she became a fashion model. Following a divorce from her first husband in 1945, she began a long-term relationship with Prince Bertil of Sweden. They lived together discreetly for thirty years and, once the Swedish succession was settled, Bertil and Lilian married in 1976, when they were both in their sixties. They always regretted that their situation made it impossible for them to have children. Lilian was an extremely popular member of the Swedish Royal Family and the patron of a number of charities. Bertil died in 1997 and Lilian continued to represent the family at official engagements until she was diagnosed with Alzheimer's disease.

2014

The BBC reported that an 82-year-old man, who had settled in Swansea after being evacuated from London in 1942 to escape the bombing, dug up an unexploded bomb in his garden at Fforestfach. He hit it twice with his spade and turned it over before he recognised what it was. An army bomb disposal team were called and promptly removed it.

24 March

1899

The *South Wales Daily Post* reported that Thomas Rowe, aged 24, appeared in court having been charged with assaulting his sister-in-law Elizabeth Thomas, a married woman, in December 1898. Elizabeth had gone to her sister's house to babysit. Her sister went out at 7 p.m. and Elizabeth put the baby to sleep on a bed – and in so doing fell asleep herself. Her brother-in-law Thomas came home later after 'drinking a little' and climbed into bed in the dark room. 'When he found somebody there he concluded it was his wife.' It was at this moment that an assault took place, but the defence decided that he had 'no guilty mind when the act was committed'. After a few minutes deliberation, the jury returned a verdict of not guilty – a verdict which was greeted by applause from the public gallery.

1941

King George V and Queen Elizabeth visited Swansea in the aftermath of the Blitz.

1943

Minutes of their meeting, held in West Glamorgan Archive, show that the Swansea Watch Committee expressed satisfaction with the work of women police auxiliaries. 'Those on street duty were doing good work but still showed a little reserve in some cases, such as going into public houses on duty. It was perhaps difficult for a woman but it was police duty.'

25 March

1807

On this day the Mumbles Railway carried the world's first fare-paying railway passengers. The tram road was originally intended to carry coal and iron ore, but it was not a success. In February 1807, the owners accepted an offer from Benjamin French of £20 per year in lieu of tolls to run passenger wagons – and history was made. Initially there were two journeys in each direction daily during the summer, a single ticket costing 1s. It began with horse power, moved on to steam and ended with electric in 1960.

1843

The French Mechanical Theatre of Arts appeared at the Assembly Rooms, Swansea. Visitors could marvel at the collection of waxworks and the 'Grand Cosmoramic Views'. This included a view of Constantinople with 'shipping passing and re-passing', and 'innumerable figures' which 'move every limb with the greatest precision'.

Admittance was '6d for Ladies and Gentlemen and 3d for working people, servants and children'.

1914

Mr Handel Davies who won a large number of prizes in South Wales last year for hill climbing, successfully negotiated Constitution Hill, Swansea, on his James cycle and side car, carrying two passengers, the three, between them weighing 30 stone. The hill is regarded as 'next to impossible,' its gradient being one in three to one in seven. For about 400 yards it averages one in five.

(*Cambrian Daily Leader*)

27 March

1841

This notice appeared in the 'Family notices' section of the *Cambrian News*: 'Died at his father's house, in the parish of Llanrhidian, Gower, Mr. John Bevan, late accountant at Mr. Thomas Walters's, Swansea. He was a young man of peaceable demeanour and strict integrity. By his own unaided exertions he had acquired considerable general knowledge.'

1976

On this date, the career of rugby player Mervyn Davies (1946–2012) ended when he suffered a subarachnoid haemorrhage and collapsed on the pitch whilst captaining Swansea against Pontypool in a Welsh Cup semi-final. He had collapsed in similar circumstances four years earlier, but at that point it had been wrongly diagnosed. He was educated at Penlan School and became a primary school teacher and one of the most significant rugby players of his time. He won his first cap for Wales in 1969 against Scotland and then played 38 consecutive matches for Wales. During this time he won two Grand Slams and three Triple Crowns, and toured New Zealand and South Africa with victorious British Lions sides in 1971 and 1974. He played 46 international matches for Wales and the Lions, and lost on only 9 occasions. He was awarded an OBE in 1976. A heavy smoker, he died of lung cancer on 15 March 2012.

29 March

1882

As part of a national tour, following success in America, Oscar Wilde appeared at the Albert Hall in Swansea. The title of his lecture was 'The House Beautiful'. It seems that he told his audience how to arrange their furniture.

1900

Dennis O'Shea, a 44-year-old fireman, was found hanging dead in his cell in Swansea Gaol by the warder Thomas Richardson after the former's conviction for manslaughter. He had hanged himself from the bars of his cell, using the cord he used to make mailbags. The judge commented that there was no evidence of any temporary insanity. O'Shea had been sentenced to five years' penal servitude after the manslaughter of Patrick Joyce, a charge he denied vehemently, particularly since there were witnesses who said that he was elsewhere. However, he was described in court as 'a notorious character' with a string of previous convictions. He had previously tried to take his own life in 1894.

1919

The *South Wales Weekly Post* announced: 'Due at Swansea for Scrapping. The twelve ex-German submarines coming to Swansea to be broken up are expected at the Swansea Ship-breaking Yard, King's Dock. Messrs. Ward and Co. have some ex-German submarines to be broken up at Briton Ferry.'

4 April

1840

The *Cambrian News* reported the inquest held on William Boundy, aged 25, a shovel-maker at the Millbrook Iron Works:

> He was turning a piece of iron for a fire poker on a lathe, when the ends of his neckerchief ... were caught by the iron while in motion, and by pressing his neck tight up to the resting piece of the lathe, caused strangulation. No person saw him until it was too late to save his life. ... The deceased was short-sighted, and consequently in working was obliged to bend forward very much. Verdict, 'Accidental Death'.

The iron works was fined 1*s*.

1867

Charles Dickens appeared in the Music Hall to give a reading from his works, which included the trial scene from *The Pickwick Papers*. It was enthusiastically received even though the majority of those present, according to the *Cambrian News*, had 'read these over and over again'. He was frequently interrupted by loud applause. 'A richer treat has seldom, if ever, been enjoyed in Swansea.'

2011

In a survey by the BBC, funeral directors reported an increase in incidents of road rage against funeral processions. One in five cortèges had been disrupted. A funeral director from Fforestfach said: 'I have had to put up with drivers hooting their horns, gesticulating rudely and using bad language.'

7 April

1865

The *Cambrian News* reported an inquest held on 'the body of a newly-born female child, the illegitimate offspring of Mary Ann Smith, a servant in a family residing in Mile End Road'. She went into labour and was taken to the workhouse in a cab. However, she had to wait for admittance and the child was born in the cab, where it died. The verdict was that the baby 'died from the want of medical assistance at birth'.

1893

Edward Phillips stabbed his wife to death in their public house, The Troubadour, in the Strand. It seems that he objected to her speaking to customers in what he regarded as a flirtatious manner. His defence claimed it was manslaughter caused by temporary insanity. He was sentenced to penal servitude for fifteen years.

1917

The South Wales Weekly Post described a 'touching ceremony' at the Tabernacle Schoolroom in Morriston, where there was a posthumous award of a Military Medal to Mrs D. Lawrence of Lower Crown Street by the mayor. She received it on behalf of her son, Oswald, who had been killed during the Somme offensive the previous year while showing 'conspicuous bravery' fighting with the Welsh Regiment. The paper noted that 'her sorrow, which was already hard to bear, had been aggravated by the loss of a second son', referring to Private Robert Lawrence, who died ten days later. Her third son had recently joined the army.

10 April

1863

It was reported in the *Cambrian News* that the Watkin family, who lived in a small cottage on Clyne Common, lost their five children very suddenly. Margaret, Ann, Richard Joanna and Elizabeth all died of diphtheria in a period of eleven days. The blame was placed upon recent wet weather after a prolonged dry spell, exacerbated by the remoteness of the house. 'The family, though poor, were much respected and the neighbours deeply sympathise with them.'

1889

Leon Pinzulu, a travelling shoemaker also known as Thomas Allen, was executed for the murder of Frederick Kent, the publican of the Gloucester Hotel in Gloucester Place. He had been hiding under Kent's bed during a robbery and had fallen asleep. When he awoke Pinzulu struck a match and, in the subsequent fight, killed Kent with a razor. He was later found hiding in the docks.

Pinzulu's execution was not a straightforward one. He was said to have had a strong neck and was seen to struggle for three minutes.

1918

Early in the morning, a tin can was thrown into a trench on the Western Front. Inside was a note. 'Dear Taffy, I have a wife within 5 miles of Swansea. What would happen if I came over to you tonight?' A prompt reply was sent. 'There would be another widow within 5 miles of Swansea tonight.' (*Cambrian Daily Leader*)

12 April

1866

This was the date of the last public execution in Swansea. It was that of Robert Coe, who had murdered John Davies with an axe at Mountain Ash. Contemporary estimates put the crowd of spectators at approximately 15,000. The night before, market traders had driven their carts right up to the gallows and removed the wheels, which they then hid so the carts could not be moved. They charged people a fee to watch the execution from a privileged position on a cart.

1870

A group of young boys was throwing stones at the windows of Vincent Street School with such enthusiasm that the teachers were trapped inside. PC 51 was called but he could only manage to detain Samuel Evans; the rest ran away. The boy was fined 10*s* with costs. (*Cambrian News*)

1907

Mary Williams, a servant from West Cross, appeared in court claiming £50 damages from Swansea dentist D.R. Jones. She claimed that during the procedure to extract four teeth, Jones had clamped open her mouth so firmly that he had dislocated her jaw, which, the defendant said, resulted in her spending seven weeks in hospital having it reset. She had been unable to speak and could take only liquids. The defence claimed that Williams was capable of dislocating her jaw at will. The judge concluded that here had not been serious negligence, merely serious consequences. He awarded damages of £15. (*Cambrian News*)

15 April

1858

The *Cambrian News* reported that Robert Sprague, a policeman, was seen in the early hours of the morning taking a tablecloth from a washing line and hiding it beneath his tunic. When questioned about it, he argued that he had taken it to keep it safe from thieves and left it in his lodgings. He went on to ask that what possible use would he, a single man, ever have for a tablecloth? He was tried in court in July 1858 where the discovery of the item hidden beneath his mattress did not help his defence. He was sent to prison for six months.

1945

Brigadier Hugh Hughes was born in Swansea in 1892. He served in the First World War as a medical officer and was awarded the DSO in 1916 for tending wounded under fire during daylight hours in no-man's-land. He also received the Military Cross and the Croix de Guerre. Hughes was promoted to brigadier during the Second World War and on this date was the first Allied medical officer to enter the concentration camp at Bergen-Belsen. He took control of the camp and was one of the main witnesses for the prosecution at the Belsen trial. In later life he became an administrator in the newly formed NHS and was Honorary Physician to the Queen. He died in Edinburgh on 24 November 1973.

18 April

1906

Morgan Williams, formerly of Catherine Street in Swansea, wrote a letter to the *Cambrian News* newspaper describing his experiences in the San Francisco earthquake. He outlined the devastation, the suffering and the distress. Williams wrote: 'It is terrible to see them getting out the bones from the ruins.' He noted that he saw the city under martial law, with looters shot. 'There was no water. The city burned for three days.' He ended his letter with an expression of regret at the form of the Swansea Town football team.

2005

The BBC reported that a Swansea man claimed to have found evidence that his ancestor, Dr Sir John Williams, was Jack the Ripper. Sir John acted as a doctor to the Royal Family and was also a founder of the National Library of Wales in Aberystwyth. It was claimed that evidence had been found linking the unsolved crimes to Sir John, which included the knife used in the five murders in London's Whitechapel district. It was suggested that he knew all five of the Ripper's victims and had even treated them. The National Library of Wales dismissed the allegations, announcing that it was proud of what its first president had achieved.

23 April

1870

The *Cardiff Times* reported an incident during a baptism at Bethesda Chapel in Swansea:

> On the appearance of the first female, a man on crutches, her husband, rushed out and declared that the ceremony should not take place, brandishing his crutches over the head of the minister. The consequences would have been very serious, but for the timely intervention of by-standers, by whom the infuriated husband was promptly secured. Further violence, or even locomotion, on the part of the husband was rendered impossible, by depriving him of his crutches.

1975

Peter Ham (b. 27 April 1947) died on this day. He was the founder of the influential group Badfinger and the writer of 'Without You', one of the notable songs of the 1970s. His group was originally called The Iveys and achieved considerable local success in Swansea before moving to London, where they were offered a recording contract by the Apple label. Their first recording, 'Come and Get It' (produced by Paul McCartney), was an international success. However, the group were financially exploited in subsequent deals with other companies and by the dubious practices of their manager. In spite of their success, band members were virtually destitute. In despair, Peter Ham took his own life just before his 28th birthday. His ashes were scattered at Morriston Crematorium and there is a commemorative plaque at High Street Station – in Ivey Place.

26 April

1889

Ludwig Wittgenstein, one of the most eminent philosophers of the twentieth century, was born in Vienna in Austria. As his academic career developed he was a frequent visitor to Swansea, where he spent holidays with his friend Rush Rhees, who taught at the university. Much of his important work *Philosophical Investigations* was written in Swansea. There are two famous photographs of Wittgenstein. One was taken in front of a blackboard in Swansea in 1947. The other is a school photograph in which he is shown as a child, apparently in the same class as Adolf Hitler.

1918

Mr. G. Knill (president of the Swansea Branch of the Typographical Society) has just returned from France after spending a few weeks with his son, Private Fred Knill, who was severely wounded in both knees, one of his legs having to be amputated. Septic poisoning has supervened, and Private Knill has been under several operations. Hopes are entertained of saving the other leg. Private Knill is progressing as favourably as possible.

(Cambrian Daily Leader)

2011

Islwyn Morris died, aged 90. He was an actor who frequently appeared in repertory in Swansea Grand Theatre, often at short notice. He also appeared as Idris in the BBC comedy series *Satellite City*. When he wasn't acting, Islwyn ran a sweet shop in the High Street Arcade.

5 May

1910

It was reported in the *South Wales Daily Post* that Nellie Burridge, aged 3, died after being admitted to Swansea Hospital with extensive burns. She had been sitting in bed playing with matches while her parents were downstairs, and set fire to her nightdress. Nellie was the third child the Burridge family had lost in the previous six months.

1939

The *South Wales Evening Post* reported a meeting held at the Bird in Hand Hotel, High Street. 'We, members of the Swansea group of Old Contemptibles, pledge ourselves to serve and form a company of the National Defence Corps. We are satisfied that the government will in no way interfere with our pensions, and in taking this step, once again wish to serve our country in case of emergency.' Men who had served in the last war were eligible to join.

2002

It was reported on the BBC website that Swansea City FC's mascot Cyril the Swan was considering a career in politics as a Welsh Assembly Member following the election of another footballing mascot, H'Angus the Monkey, as Mayor of Hartlepool in local elections. Cyril's election pledge to the voters was that he would donate his salary to the football club.

1843

The warehouse of sailmakers Mrs Couch & Sons caught fire in the early hours. 'In a short time the powerful first class engine of the Norwich Fire Insurance Office, which is kept in a shed at the station-house, was procured ... and commenced pouring a plentiful supply of water upon the buildings.' However, the fire spread to Beynon's warehouse, which was filled with combustible materials including, it was rumoured, several tons of gunpowder. 'We need hardly say that the quantity was immensely exaggerated but ... it deterred several persons from taking as active a part as they otherwise would in the suppression of the flames.' The Hafod fire engine also arrived and the fire was brought under control.

1958

Vivian Frederick Teed, 24, of Manor Road in Manselton, beat 73-year-old William Williams to death with twenty-seven blows from a hammer at the sub-post office in Fforestfach during a robbery. In spite of strong evidence suggesting 'impaired mental responsibility', Teed was found guilty of murder and sentenced to death. He was hanged at 9.00 a.m. on this day in Swansea Prison, the last man to be executed there.

2004

The *South Wales Evening Post* was pleased to confirm that a hamster reported stolen in a break-in at a flat in Siloh Road in Landore was later found running around the property. It was in fact a CD player that had been taken.

10 May

1866

A serious fire destroyed Mr John's draper's shop at No. 2 Temple Street, killing eight people. Sadly there was considerable delay in obtaining the town ladder, since it was locked in the castle yard and the key had been lost. The fire engine was brought out, but the hoses made little impact on the blaze, which burned for three hours. As a consequence a new fire escape ladder was purchased for the town to be kept in an accessible location. It came from Preston and cost £45, with an additional carriage charge of a guinea.

1898

The Mumbles Pier was opened on this day. It cost £10,000 and was over 250 yards long.

1918

During an assault on Aveluy Wood in Lancashire towards the end of the First World War, twelve members of the Swansea Battalion were killed and thirty wounded in a 'friendly fire' incident, the result of misdirected shelling from British Artillery Units.

1955

On this day an episode of the BBC Radio comedy *Hancock's Half Hour* featuring Tony Hancock called 'Visit to Swansea' was broadcast. Harry Secombe appeared as guest star. Sadly the recording has not survived and is considered lost.

11 May

1888

There was a great deal of ill feeling during a strike at the Elba Steel Works in Gowerton. Philip Lewis, a furnace man, had gone back to work while industrial action was still being taken.

At 3.30 a.m., a bomb was thrown into his house. There was a loud explosion but no serious damage, other than blackening of the furniture. The remains of a sock and a ginger beer bottle with a fuse were recovered from the scene. Lewis had previously been assaulted by a gang of women for being a blackleg.

1948

Although Swansea tradesmen made provisions to deal with possible queues when they opened following the change in rationing arrangements for clothes and shoes, there was 'little enthusiasm displayed by the public'. The *South Wales Evening Post* reported that 'an hour after opening, most clothes shops were empty.' However, 'there was demand for children's shoes, now obtainable without coupons but most of the mothers were anxious to buy white shoes for the children for Whitsun. Most of the shops had not enough stock to cope with demand.' A tradesman was reported as saying: 'It suggests to me that there is not a great deal of money about these days.'

2005

The last match at Vetch Field took place when Swansea beat Wrexham 2–1 in the Football Association of Wales Premier Cup Final.

13 May

1906

A thunderstorm broke over Morriston. Heavy rain started at midday, rendering streets impassable and bringing traffic to a complete halt. The thunder continued and during the evening service in one chapel, '4 or 5 women were carried out in a fainting condition'. (*The Daily Post*)

1916

The *Cambrian Daily Leader* reported that at a meeting of the Royal Institution in Swansea, Sir J. Thompson spoke of an idea that had been forwarded to him:

> The inventor had apparently observed that birds will peck mortar and so suggested that a flock of cormorants— chosen presumably because of their great appetites—should be trained to feed by putting their food in horizontal and vertical lines against a wall. They were then to be taken to Essen and liberated to attack the great chimneys at Krupps works with such vigour as to destroy them.

2008

The BBC reported that a Swansea motorist had been trapped in her car by a flying mattress. The driver's small hatchback drove over a double mattress, which had fallen from the back of a van, becoming stuck with its wheels on either side, off the ground. Police and two ambulance crews were called to Walter Road after the driver was trapped and appeared to be in shock. The van, meanwhile, had disappeared towards Uplands. Police were unable to trace the driver.

29 May

1869

Henry F. Love was charged with unlawfully trying to collect donations for the Cambrian Institution for the Deaf and Dumb. He visited shops with false identification, pretending to be profoundly deaf and requesting money in writing.

1896

It was reported in the *Cambrian News* that there had been a 'painful affair' outside a sweet shop at the corner of High Street and Greyhound Street. A large group of children were playing outside the shop and causing what the owner John Powe perceived to be a nuisance. In an attempt to move them on, he threw some water over them. One of them fetched his mother, Sarah Jones, who turned up to complain. There was – inevitably – an argument, during which Powe grabbed a pan and threw the contents over her. However, it wasn't water. It was boiling sugar. Sarah was taken to hospital and an angry crowd quickly gathered outside the shop and smashed its windows. The paper noted that 'it was with great difficulty that the police arrested and took Powe to the police station'. Once he had gone, his premises were looted.

The case appeared in court and Powe was bound over in the sum of £50 to keep the peace. Sarah Jones recovered from the burns, explaining that it wasn't so bad; some of the marks on her face had been caused earlier by smallpox.

30 May

1873

George Smith and Arthur Stevens, furnace men at the Copper Works in Morriston, were charged with absenting themselves from their work without leave, causing considerable loss to their employers, who claimed £9 11s 6d in compensation. The defendants did not deny they left work without permission, but pleaded that they were ill; they admitted however that they had not obtained a medical certificate as required. The magistrates said the case had been fully proved, and they ordered the defendants to pay the amount claimed between them (£4 15s 9d each) and the costs – or serve a month's imprisonment.

(Cambrian News)

1907

The drowned body of Sarah Jane Stevens was recovered from the River Tawe. She was 'neatly dressed' according to the *Cambrian News*, and was found lying on a mudbank. She was 19 years old and in service with the Siedle family at 51 Walter Road. Her parents lived on Bonymaen Road in Pentrechwyth. It was discovered that Mrs Siedle had decided to terminate her employment. Apparently, 'she was of poor intelligence but she did not take orders as she should', which Mrs Siedle put down to disobedience. Sarah disappeared later the same night as receiving notice. The verdict of the inquest was that she had been 'found drowned'.

2011

Swansea City beat Reading 4–2 in the Championship Play-Off final to gain promotion to the Premier League for the first time.

31 May

1845

The inquest was held on George Gibbs of Overton, Port Eynon, who died painfully from what his doctor described as constipation. However, a post-mortem suggested that he had been poisoned with corrosive sublimate. His son was implicated but nothing could be proved and so the inquest returned a verdict of 'died by the visitation of God'.

1856

The staff at the Duke of Wellington Inn in Swansea were awakened in the early hours by a disturbance on the roof during a storm. They called the police, who brought a ladder and recovered a man dressed in 'a nightcap, night shirt and drawers' who was 'drenched to the skin'. Although the man claimed to have been robbed, he was found to be from Tredegar and a guest at the Castle Hotel. It seemed that he had opened his bedroom window and sleepwalked across the roofs of Swansea, 'encountering dangers perfectly appalling to everyone but a somnambulist'. (*The Monmouthshire Merlin*)

1878

Richard Rees, aged 10, was charged with 'depositing nuisance on the beach'. He claimed he had been told to do it by his employer, and was discharged with a caution. John Jones and Albert Watts were also charged with committing a similar offence on the same date. Jones pleaded ignorance and was fined 5*s*. Watts, who had been previously cautioned, was fined 10*s*.

1 June

1855

The *Monmouth Merlin and Silurian* announced: 'We have the painful duty to-day to record the death of the Rev. David Edwards of Swansea who was drowned a few days since at Liverpool.' Prior to his departure for America on the *Miles Barton*, it seems that Edwards got into 'doubtful company, no doubt being allured by what are termed in Liverpool "Man Catchers", with which the port abounds. It would seem that these harpies succeeded in inducing the deceased to partake freely of intoxicating beverages, it is supposed with the view of ultimately robbing him, but whether they were successful in the disgraceful plot has not been satisfactorily ascertained.' When boarding the ship, Edwards fell off the gangway into the water, striking his head against the side of both the wharf and the ship and drowning.

1880

French engineer and builder of the Suez Canal, Ferdinand de Lesseps, visited Swansea. The mayor invited him to what the *Cambrian News* was pleased to describe as 'dejeuner' at the Mackworth Arms Hotel. His purpose was to explain the 'value and utility of the proposed Panama Canal scheme to South Wales merchants and shippers'. The following day, de Lesseps was due to speak on the same topic in Amsterdam. Construction of the canal began in 1881, but the project went bankrupt and was abandoned. The United States restarted work in 1904.

6 June

1887

William Gladstone arrived in Swansea for what the *Cambrian News* described as 'a few days' rest and retirement'. He was initially taken on a drive through 'Gowerland', but it was not all relaxation. A number of speeches were given. He opened the new Public Library on Alexandra Road with a golden key, presented to him in a velvet case by William Williams, jewellers of Castle Street. He also received a piece of coal (mounted by William Williams) from local miners and a steel woodman's axe.

1902

A number of Swansea men were on board the steamship *Roddam* in St Pierre, Martinique, when the volcano erupted. Reports in the *Western Mail* told of red-hot dust falling on them whilst the sea boiled. The marks of the feet of seamen could be seen on the deck where their skin had burnt off. The chief engineer, Mr Watters from Swansea, was killed. He was found on deck, his clothes burnt, his moustache completely disappeared and his scalp and hair 'shrivelled off'. The second mate also died later in hospital.

1903

Ceri Richards (1903–1971), painter and print-maker, was born in Dunvant. He studied engineering draughtsmanship and drawing in Swansea and later in London. He went on to lead the painting department at Cardiff School of Art. His work includes paintings and lithographs to illustrate the work of Welsh writers such as Dylan Thomas and Vernon Watkins.

8 June

1765

Silvanus Bevan died in Hackney on this day. He had been born in Swansea in 1691 to a family of prosperous Quakers (his father was also called Silvanus). Bevan became a notable apothecary on Oxford Street in London and then practised 'physic' in Hackney, becoming a member of the Royal Society in 1725, as proposed by Isaac Newton. In retirement he took an interest in the creation of the first hospital in Philadelphia.

1918

William Jones, a barber, was charged in Swansea with unlawfully supplying a drug to Henry Brown 'to enable him to render himself, or induce the belief that he was, unfit for military service'. Sadly for Jones his latest client, Brown, was part of an elaborate trap. Jones had been set up by the police, who had been tracking him for selling pills to those keen to avoid being called up to the forces. He was charging £5 and offering complete satisfaction or your money back. When he tried to do a deal with Brown, the waiting police pounced. Subsequent analysis showed that the pills contained around 40 per cent nitroglycerine and were 'dangerous to the heart'. Jones was sentenced to six months in prison.

1940

In anticipation of air raids, the council purchased fifty washable, reusable canvas coffins with solid removable bases at a total cost of £50. A lorry with a canvas hood was bought and sites for temporary mortuaries identified.

9 June

1804

The *Cambrian News* reported a horrific incident during the celebrations for King George IV's birthday. Troops were firing a salute on Swansea Burrows. The first volley was entirely successful but Captain Jones called for the second too soon, whilst John Griffiths, 'an old Gunner', was still ramming additional wadding into the barrel of one of the guns. He was 'in an instant rendered a most shocking spectacle'. His left arm was ripped off and flew about 40 yards; his face was 'dreadfully disfigured' and he sustained a large wound on his left side. He survived only a few moments. A collection was held for his widow and five children.

1827

'An explosion of fire-damp took place in a colliery in Llansamlet by which three men unfortunately lost their lives. We are credibly informed that the proprietor has furnished the colliery with the Davy lamp but the men, with fatal obstinacy to their own safety, neglect to use them.' (*Cambrian News*)

1899

Henry Pelican, a German seaman, stabbed William Kingdom to death in Baptist Court, 'one of the narrowest and dirtiest alleys in Swansea'. Pelican was in the house of prostitute Ellen Waltham when he argued with her partner, Kingdom. Pelican claimed that he had acted in self-defence. He was acquitted.

15 June

1835

A huge thunderstorm revealed a collection of Roman coins that were found by a young girl near Pentrechwyth. It became known as the 'Gwindy Horde' and contained coins from the third century AD. They were probably in a grave, but in their haste local people threw any bones away and smashed the jar that held the coins.

1849

'A large quantity of sheet lead has lately been stolen from the roof of the Townhall by some evil-disposed person. The authorities have issued a notice offering £5 reward for such information as will lead to the apprehension and conviction of the offenders.' (*Cambrian News*)

1877

There was a fatal accident involving Thomas Wilmot, a hammerman at the steel works. The machine he was operating malfunctioned and he was struck by the hammer on the forehead, causing his skull to be cut open. He was taken home and died soon afterwards. He was 32 years old.

Thomas was buried in the Bethlehem Chapel grounds in Fforestfach. However, on this day a letter appeared in the *Cambrian News*, saying that his friends believed he had had a premonition of death. On the day of the accident he had been gloomy and had told everyone that something 'strange' was going to happen.

19 June

1899

Barnum and Bailey, proprietors of 'The Greatest Show on Earth', arrived at the Victoria Park Grounds. The show was described in advertising as 'truthful, moral, instructive'. A ticket gave access to everything in the multitude of marquees – such as the menagerie, the shows and the 'collection of freaks'. Visitors could meet Hassan Ali, the tallest man in the world, the dwarfs Khusama and Delphi and 'fire-brand tossing seals' amongst so many attractions. An estimated crowd of 20,000 turned up. The company reportedly paid £50 for the hire of the park; their takings were estimated at £7,000.

1908

Under the headline 'Poverty to Wealth', the *Western Mail* announced the death of James Brazil, known as 'Jimmy the Brace'. He lived his later years in humble circumstances in Greenhill but had made a fortune from investments, initially in gold mining in Australia and latterly in Canadian railways. Although he remained largely illiterate, he made his money from buying and selling stocks and shares. He lived off stale bread with no butter because it was cheaper and left a legacy of about £80,000. Jimmy did buy houses, however, which he gave to the local priest to allocate, but generally, if people asked him for money, he would usually reply, 'What's the point? You would only spend it.'

It seems that a long-lost nephew heard that he was unwell and took him away to Ireland, where he died a few weeks later.

25 June

1675

During armed conflict between European colonists and Native Americans, a band of Pokanoket Indians attacked the settlement of Swansea in Massachusetts. They laid siege to the village for five days before destroying it completely on 25 June 1675.

1915

Beneath the headline 'Shot in the Dardanelles', the *Cambrian Daily Leader* printed an extract from a soldier's letter:

> I expect by this time you have seen my name in the casualty list. I was wounded in the back, and the bullet has lodged somewhere inside – in the stomach, I think by the pain I have had in that region. I was making tea at the time and had crawled out of the dug-out to put the tea in the 'dixie' when I was caught bending by a sniper. It was a splendid shot, and being hit in a 'tender spot', I shall not be able to sit down for some time.

2011

A man threw a bone at friends standing on the central reservation in Carmarthen Road after buying chicken pieces in Fforestfach. As he did so, a police officer in an unmarked car used by the CID made an emergency stop to arrest him and four cars behind were badly damaged when they also had to brake. A number of people suffered minor injuries. The man who admitted throwing the bone was conditionally discharged and ordered to pay £85 court costs. Fortunately, the police car was undamaged.

27 June

1287

Oystermouth Castle was burnt during the rebellion of Rhys ap Maredudd. 'Certain men who were captured Rhys caused to be strangled before his eyes, others he led away captive. He violated the church for the sake of loot and slew the wives and children of the men indifferently.'

1940

The first air raid on Swansea during the Second World War happened at 3.30 a.m. on Danygraig Road. Six bombs were dropped, four of which failed to explode.

1942

The South Wales District Committee of the Communist Party complained that their meeting, held in the YMCA on St Helen's Road, had been bugged by the police. They found an inexpertly hidden microphone and wires leading to an adjacent room, where a police notebook was found containing accurate notes of their meeting. The police declined to comment.

1946

Muriel Drinkwater, aged just 12, was murdered in the woods at Penllergaer as she made her way home from school. She was raped, beaten around the head, shot twice in the chest and left lying in the bushes. The murderer has never been identified.

1 July

1815

The following report appeared in the *Cambrian News*:

> A melancholy accident happened on Sunday evening last while the Milford and Bristol Mail was on its road to Swansea. About six miles from thence, the driver, George Masters, fell from the box, it is supposed in a fit, and was taken up dead. Fortunately no accident occurred by the temporary freedom which the horses obtained.

1910

The decomposed body of a female child was discovered in the parcels office at High Street station. A woman who had arrived on the London train had deposited the brown paper package the previous day. Staff were alerted by the smell. The child had been dead for about ten days and had been wrapped in pages from a London weekly newspaper. The woman who paid the charge of 2*d* was never traced.

1915

The *Cambrian News* interviewed Private Crawford, 21, of the Royal Welsh Fusiliers who had been sent home to Swansea to recuperate from his wounds:

> The rotten part about it was the fact that I was not in action, really. While our men were engaging the enemy I was employed carrying provisions into the trenches about 30 yards behind. Suddenly I felt a pain in the stomach, and I found that a bullet had gone right through me and had killed a little terrier that was unlucky enough to be right behind me.

7 July

1898

Maggie O'Neill was stabbed to death by her husband Henry with a pocketknife at their home in Powell Street. Henry had been dismissed from his job at the Vivian works in Hafod due to ill health, and had then gone to sea on the ship *Para*, which became shipwrecked in ice off Newfoundland. The crew had been picked up by the *Marina*, which also became briefly trapped in ice. It was felt that he had suffered significant mental trauma as a result, which was the reason behind his unprovoked assault on his wife. After killing Maggie, Henry drowned himself in the canal.

1941

Michael Howard, British Conservative politician, was born in Gorseinon to a Romanian father and Russian mother. He was a student at Llanelli Boys' Grammar School and at Peterhouse, at Cambridge University before being called to the Bar at the Inner Temple in 1964, specialising in employment and planning law. He was first elected to Parliament in 1983 for Folkestone and Hythe and held a number of senior Cabinet posts, including that of Home Secretary. For two years (2003–2005), Howard was leader of the Conservative party and Leader of the Opposition. He also employed David Cameron as a Special Advisor. He stood down at the 2010 election and became Baron Howard of Lympne, a Conservative life peer in the House of Lords.

11 July

1811

This was the birth date of Sir William Grove, the pioneer of fuel cell technology. He is known for developing the Grove Cell in 1839, which produced electricity through zinc and platinum electrodes exposed to acids, as well as inventing the first incandescent light. His work influenced other scientists like Faraday, Edison and Joule. Grove was knighted in 1872 and died in 1896. Grove Place in Swansea was named after him.

1934

The father of 39-year-old Frederick Symons from Swansea, who drowned in the Serpentine in Hyde Park, stated at the inquest that his son seemed to have a peculiar brain: he could do two things at the same time. 'He could do his work and still carry on a conversation about something else. A verdict of suicide while of unsound mind was returned.' (*Taunton Courier*)

1946

The Evening Post reported a failed robbery at the Swansea Grand Cinema. While several hundred people were enjoying Paulette Goddard's performance in *I Love a Soldier*, Hugh Davies, an ex-serviceman 'with his face heavily masked with bandages' threatened the manager, saying 'Stick 'em up. I have a gun in my pocket.' The manager, Bob Turton, replied, 'You are not going to get away with this,' and punched him on the jaw. 'He went down and I jumped on him and called for help.' The police found in Davies' pocket 'a small hammer which he had used to represent a gun'.

12 July

1810

'At a village called Llansamlet during a storm, about 40 persons were induced to seek shelter in a mill, which being struck by the lightning, killed three men and wounded about twenty others. The miller who was at work, escaped, but the mill was burnt down to the ground.' (*Cheltenham Chronicle and Gloucestershire General Advertiser*)

1896

It was with great excitement that the *Cambrian News* reported that 'new photography was successfully applied for the purposes of surgical operation'. A woman had the point of a needle embedded in her palm, but its exact position could not be determined. Rontgen Rays were generated by Bunsen burners connected to a coil and a Newton bulb, and the afflicted hand was placed on a photographic plate. The exposure time was twenty minutes. The needle point was clearly seen and there will be 'little difficulty in extracting the unpleasant stranger'.

1940

A letter from Mr Evans in Tycoch was received by the Town Clerk's office, reporting damage to his car during an air raid on the King's Dock. The car had been removed to the garage of B.J. Rees on Oxford Street, who would write a report on the extent of the damage. Mr Evans requested 'the necessary forms' so that he could claim compensation.

14 July

1893

Stallholders in Swansea market complained of an enormous increase in the number of rats that were emerging from the sewers in Orange Street. These 'cunning and somewhat fearsome creatures' were causing huge damage. Meat was eaten and generally spoiled. Although it was hung from hooks in the ceiling, 'the rats formed themselves into a string, hanging on to each other so that the lowest could get at the meat'. (*Cambrian News*)

1903

The Buffalo Bill Wild West Show arrived in Swansea. It arrived at East Dock station early in the morning after their previous appearance in Llanelli. Around 2,000 people from St Thomas were already there to see the 'cowboys, the Indians, the Deadwood Stage, the laughing Gauchos and the Cossacks'. Over 800 people travelled with the show, along with 560 horses. A procession like 'a leaf out of romance made its way smartly through the prosaic streets of St Thomas' to a marquee erected at Victoria Park. A great number of visitors arrived to see the shows, with special trains running from the Swansea Valley and the Rhondda. 'Many of the works are closed in order to allow the workmen to see Colonel Cody's great show.' (*Cambrian News*)

17 July

1914

A tattooed body was washed up on the beach at Jersey Marine. It was 'devoid of clothing' but the arms bore a tattooed crucifix and the initials 'JW'.

1939

Spencer Davis, founder of the 1960s rock band The Spencer Davis Group, was born in Swansea and attended Dynevor School, becoming head boy in 1959. In 1960 he went to the University of Birmingham to study German. The quartet he went on to form had No. 1 hits with consecutive single releases in 1966 ('Keep on Running' and 'Somebody Help Me') with Steve Winwood on lead vocals. A long-term supporter of Plaid Cymru, Davis lives on Catalina Island, a small island off the coast of southern California.

1948

Edgar Davies, a 43-year-old carpenter, was found guilty of putting rat poison in his wife's tea. When he discovered that she could taste it, he put it in seven bottles of medicine his wife Doris had received from her doctor. However, she was clearly suspicious by this time and the fumes the poison gave off made Doris aware something was wrong. When sentencing Davies to three years' penal servitude, Justice Denning told him: 'This was a most wicked attempt by you to murder your wife simply because you have your eyes set on another woman. She was a good wife to you and you said she was touchy.' (*Daily Mail*)

20 July

1664

Innkeepers Thomas and Marie John were granted the apprenticeship of a 9-year-old pauper by the Overseers of the Poor. His name was Thomas Mantle and he was to remain with them for twelve years, after which the Johns were to provide him with 'two sufficient suits of apparel fitt for an apprentice of his estate and degree'. Thomas John received a fee of 50*s* (quoted in W.C. Rogers, *Historic Swansea*).

1966

Cecilia Owens, who died on this day aged 87, survived the sinking of the RMS *Lusitania* off the coast of Ireland on 7 May 1915. The liner was hit by a single torpedo fired from a German submarine. Almost everyone else in her family party – including her husband and two sons – was lost, on their way to visit Swansea from where they had emigrated. Cecilia went back to America but eventually returned to Swansea and died in the city in 1966. The only other member of the party to survive was her 6-year-old niece, Helen. She too had been born in Swansea, in 1908, before emigrating. Helen lost her parents and brother and after the disaster lived in Swansea with her mother's family. She worked in a shoe shop, married John Thomas and had a daughter called Elizabeth. Helen died aged 84 on 8 April 1993.

21 July

1904

King Edward VII and Queen Alexandra left Swansea after including the town in their tour of Wales. On his previous visit as Prince of Wales in 1881, Edward had opened the Prince of Wales Dock. This time he cut the first sod in the construction of the King's Dock. It was completed in 1909 and is still the principal dock in Swansea. During his visit he spoke to old soldiers, including John Lear, who served in the Crimea, and to David Jenkins, who claimed to have fought at Rorke's Drift in 1879.

1905

Several complaints were received by the police about sheep-worrying on Kilvey Hill. A sheep was found at the bottom of a quarry with all of its legs broken, having been attacked by stray dogs. A lamb was also discovered in the quarry, injured after falling whilst being chased by the same dogs.

1992

A postcard written by William Rogers was sold at Sotheby's. The RMS *Titanic* postcard was written in pencil to his friend James Day in Swansea. It was posted in Queenstown, Ireland, on 11 April 1912. It said: 'Just a line to show that I am alive and kicking going grand it's a treat.'

26 July

1817

John Gill was mooring his boat in Swansea Harbour. As he threw out the anchor that was resting on his shoulder, one of the flukes caught his neck and he was dragged overboard and drowned. His father had been drowned on the same day twenty years previously, in 1797. (*Cambrian News*)

1897

Swansea Grand Theatre was formally opened by Madame Adelina Patti, a leading soprano and eccentric of the time who lived at Craig y Nos. The theatre was built on the site of the Drill Hall in Singleton Street and the opening is commemorated by a plaque still visible in the auditorium. The first performance, which did not take place until a few days later, was the Japanese opera *The Geisha*.

1993

Concern was expressed about the number of accidents involving pedestrians on the Kingsway. Many incidents involved 'late-night drinkers and club-goers weaving their way across regardless of traffic'. In the previous three years, one person had been killed and eighty-eight injured, usually at night. A number of measures were suggested to 'reduce the carnage'. These included the installation of pelican crossings, the erection of barriers on the central reservation along with raised plant beds and guardrails on the pavement. An editorial in the *Evening Post* welcomed the news as a sensible step for safety and as 'the first stage in the pedestrianisation of the road'.

7 August

1891

Beneath the headline 'The Drunken Draggle-Tailed Wives of Swansea', the *Cambrian News* expressed concern over the levels of female drunkenness in Swansea, which resulted in 'impoverishment' and the 'degradation of home life'. The reporter commented upon the 'offensive filthiness of women and children' and reflected on a downward spiral of neglect – of men driven to drink by the 'unattractiveness of their homes and by the foolishness, if not indeed the foulness of their wives'. This in turn bred the neglect that drove women to drink.

1914

There were protests in Swansea about local traders increasing their prices with the outbreak of war. People gathered in the High Street and some windows were broken with stones. 'As the demonstrations approached Oxford Street the numbers swelled until traffic was almost impassable.' The crowd was excitable, alternately singing 'Rule Britannia' and 'The Red Flag'. Traders who hadn't raised prices were cheered.

There was a particularly tense atmosphere on Prince of Wales Road, where Mr Price had increased the price of lump sugar by 4*d* a pound. His shop windows were smashed at midnight, whilst those of Trevor Evans two doors away were untouched because he had not increased his prices. By this time there were allegedly 'thousands' demonstrating and mounted police were called to disperse the crowd. A policeman named Gwilym was injured by flying glass.

8 August

1812

The following notice was published in the *Cambrian News*:

> Runaway apprentice. Absconded from his master's service, (William Spring, Cabinet maker, Swansea) on the 3rd inst. JOHN WHITE, aged 19, about five feet six inches high; had on when he absconded a fustian jacket and trousers. Whoever harbours or employs the said John White, shall be proceeded against according to law.

1914

Eighty-five German seamen had been detained in Swansea at the outbreak of war and housed initially in school buildings at Rutland Street. On this day they were marched to High Street station and departed for Queensferry near Chester where, the *Cambrian News* was pleased to announce, 'a concentration camp had been formed'. Meanwhile, it was alleged that a foreign resident of Swansea had cut off one of his fingers to prevent being called up for his country's military service. He was not prepared to fight against Britain, which he now regarded as his home.

1977

Warren Mitchell appeared at Swansea Grand Theatre in his one-man show, *The Thoughts of Chairman Alf*, in which he adopted the persona of reactionary TV character Alf Garnett. During the performance a member of the audience, incensed by his views on 'women's lib', began heckling. He jumped on stage and attacked the actor, hitting him on the side of the head, before being escorted from the theatre.

17 August

1904

Weaver & Co. Ltd of North Dock was charged with a breach of the Factory Act by not having machinery properly fenced following a fatal accident. A young boy called William Burns was standing on a platform to connect a belt when he was caught by the strap of a pulley and 'so carried round and killed. The erection of the platform had brought the machinery within a dangerous distance.' Despite the fact that the mill manager claimed William was standing in the wrong place, it was established that there was no protection at all. The company was fined £20. (*Cambrian News*)

1906

It was reported in the *Cambrian News* that a Swansea man had been eaten by a crocodile. William Warman was working on the railway in Salisbury, Rhodesia, and was coming to the end of his six-year contract. While crossing the Kafue River, his raft was overturned by a crocodile, which seized Warman and disappeared with him. He was never seen again. Warman had previously worked on the Midland Railway at the Foxhole signal box and had lived on Sebastopol Street in St Thomas.

2005

In the first international football match held at the Liberty Stadium, Wales and Slovenia drew 0–0.

18 August

1900

The *Western Mail* published a letter from someone using the name 'Consideration':

> As you are aware there is 'Little Langland Bay' in Langland. This has always borne the title of 'ladies bay,' and is given up to ladies and children for bathing, who are prohibited, properly, from the gentlemen's portion of the bay. But now, gentlemen very imperfectly clad, use the ladies bay, and with a complete indifference to the feelings of visitors.

The writer asks for the erection of signs identifying the area for the exclusive use of ladies during the morning.

1905

George Edwards and his daughter Caroline were summoned for assaulting Ann, George's wife and Caroline's mother. Ann claimed that George struck her on the arm with a poker, and that Caroline beat her with a chair. Ann asserted repeatedly that George was the father of Caroline's child and went on to accuse Caroline of cruelty, saying that the latter had thrown pepper into the baby's eyes. The case against Caroline was dismissed. According to George, 'it's gone unbearable. To say that an old man like me is the father of that child, I can't stand it. I did hit her.' The mayor replied: 'You are a man of years and you ought to know better than to take up a poker to your wife. You are fined 20*s* or 14 days.'

'Well sir, I'll go down,' said Edwards.

19 August

1896

On this day, the notorious Swansea character Ellen Sweeney died in the workhouse, where she had been ill for two months with 'enlargement of the liver', according to the *Cambrian News*. She was about 63 years old and had appeared in court on 278 occasions, usually for being drunk and disorderly. In the end the court abandoned the usual gaol sentence and sent her to the workhouse, where she became an almost permanent resident.

Ellen was born in Swansea and had a child at 15 years of age. Her first conviction came soon afterwards for theft and it was then that she started drinking. She spent most of her life in prison on short sentences, and was regarded as the best laundress they ever had. On her release she would go into a public house, order a drink and threaten to smash all the windows unless she received it for nothing.

She left all her effects to the undertaker to provide for her funeral. The sale of her assets realised £1 18s and she was buried in Danygraig Cemetery. The newspaper ended its report with 'Poor Ellen. We will miss her.'

1910

William Green, a retired draper from Norton, died whilst watering his kidney beans. He had gone out on to the top of his bay window to water beans that were growing up the wall but fell to the pavement below and died instantly.

23 August

1895

The *Cambrian News* reported that Edwin Louden had returned to Swansea. He had suffered a total physical collapse in Algiers after abandoning his attempt to walk round the world, while his companion, Herbert Field, had abandoned the venture in January. They were known as the 'Swansea Pedestrians' and they had planned to fund the adventure by working as they went. They hoped to be in Tibet by 1897 and to eventually produce an illustrated book. However, the only work they could find when arriving in France was cleaning knives in a kitchen, polishing shoes and harvesting potatoes. In November they 'arrived in Paris with 10*d* and very hearty appetites'. By the time he arrived in Algiers, Edwin had walked through France, Spain and Portugal, covering 2,200 miles 'unfrequented by tourists'. The *Cambrian News* ended by saying that he was a 'shadow of his former self ... Swansea's indifference to [his] welfare has been very unkind.'

2005

A Swansea pet shop began a Rent-a-Hamster scheme, which would help parents ascertain whether their children were ready for the responsibilities of pet ownership. The hamster, called Freddie, was delivered together with cage, food, bedding, and care manual. 'Some will rent a hamster from us again and again, particularly during the school holidays.' Since the lifespan of a hamster is about two years, Freddie was the third hamster available for rent, following Daisy and Freckles. (BBC)

29 August

1773

On this day, the first rents were paid by the residents of 'Morris Castle'. This is now the iconic ruin that sits above Landore and has come to represent the east side of Swansea. It was built by John Morris to house the families of his workers and the building is regarded as the first block of workers' flats, constructed around an internal quadrangle. Today only the corners remain – the spaces between them were once filled with three-storey buildings, the fireplaces and windows of which can still be identified. False battlements made of copper slag topped the buildings. They had a form of central heating and centralised refuse disposal, using chutes from the upper floors. They were intended to house about forty families but were never popular with residents, not least because of the lack of access to water. It had to be carried up the hill and then up the stairs. The flats were occupied until about 1850, when nearby mining made the structure unsafe.

1806

It was reported in the *Cambrian News* that David George was clearing his net after fishing when he saw a small sole entangled in the mesh. He put the head of the fish between his teeth to draw it through the net – a common practice, apparently. However, the fish slipped into his throat and David promptly choked to death.

31 August

1855

Lewis Weston Dillwyn, owner of The Cambrian Pottery, died in Sketty Hall. He was a naturalist and published work on botany and shells. He also wrote a short but important history of Swansea in 1840, served as MP for Glamorgan, was elected Mayor of Swansea and was one of the founders of the Royal Institution of South Wales.

1888

Revd Mr Lloyd from the Unitarian Chapel on High Street was exploring Long Hole, a cave in Gower, when he found a mammoth tooth weighing almost 2lbs.

1968

Gary Sobers, captain of Nottinghamshire County Cricket team, hit six sixes in one over at St Helens whilst playing against Glamorgan. The unfortunate bowler was Malcolm Nash, who had recently changed his bowling style from medium pace to left-arm spin. At the time, Sobers was the first batsman to achieve this feat. Sobers was caught off the fifth delivery by Roger Davies, who fell backwards over the boundary, thus invalidating the catch. The ball was sold at auction in November 2006 for £26,400, though some, like Nash himself, do not believe that it is authentic. Nash was also hit for five sixes and a four in one over by Frank Hayes of Lancashire in 1977. Nash once hit four consecutive sixes himself but it is his association with Sobers' batting for which he will always be remembered.

2 September

1910

The police arrived to dig up the garden of No. 136 Eaton Road in Brynhyfryd. The new tenant of the property was planting cabbages when he began to unearth coffins. (Local residents later commented that they saw 'horrible shovels-full'.) Eventually the badly decomposed bodies of sixteen babies were found, making identification impossible. It was a 'baby cemetery'.

The previous occupant of the house had been Frederick Pegler, an undertaker. Local women had brought their babies to him and paid to have them buried in the cemetery, but he had instead buried them in his garden. Pegler had been declared bankrupt in April and had gone to work at sea.

It was decided that his actions were not criminal in themselves, though individual parents could have taken a case out against Pegler for not delivering the service they had paid for. Pegler could not be contacted and the babies were interred at Danygraig Cemetery at public expense.

1941

'A letter was read and discussed from the Gower Local Savings Committee. As Gower was not able to organise a Special War Weapons Week each savings group is asked to set itself a special objective in the form of a weapon. The committee offers the suggestion of endeavouring to cover the cost of a machine gun, cost £100.' (The minutes of the Reynoldston Women's Institute)

11 September

1941

This was the date of the death of Henry Grindell Matthews. He was a strange and unusual character, an engineer and inventor from Gloucestershire who claimed to have developed a mysterious radio ray that could bring all traffic to a halt. In his final years he worked in his mountain laboratory at Tor Clawdd, above Rhydypandy, on a submarine detection system. His most notable – and verifiable – achievement was developing the system for recording sound directly on to film, and he was the first man to transmit spoken messages from the ground to planes in flight. Many of his other claims became increasingly outlandish and he revelled in his newspaper reputation as 'Death Ray Matthews'. The story that he held frequent meetings during the early part of the war with Winston Churchill in the Mason's Arms Public House in Rhydypandy to discuss security issues is unfounded.

2001

There were two known victims of the al-Quaeda attack on the World Trade Center who were born in Swansea. One was Nicholas John, aged 42 from Dunvant, who worked for Chase Manhattan Bank and was attending a meeting in the building that day. The other was Kathryn Wolf, aged 37. Her maiden name was James and she had lived in West Cross, attending Bishop Gore School. She had originally been an accomplished classical pianist who later became a Wall Street financier.

22 September

1876

Albert Cox was charged with cruelly ill-treating a donkey. Policeman Smith saw the prisoner in charge of a donkey attached to a cart carrying meat:

> He was standing up in the cart with the reins in his left hand, and a meat tray in his right with which he struck the animal violently on the back four times, which made the donkey crouch down in the shafts. He was fined 10*s* or seven days. The Stipendiary said he wished to take this opportunity of stating that he was at present staying at the Caswell Hotel, and he saw a great deal of cowardly and heartless cruelty by boys who drove the donkeys. On the previous day there was one animal being kicked in front of the hotel. If the matter were mentioned in the papers it might have the effect of putting a stop to the cruelty now practised.
>
> (*Cambrian Daily Leader*)

1952

Laurel and Hardy appeared at the Empire Theatre on Oxford Street. They stayed in the Mackworth Hotel on High Street and often sat on the balcony waving at their fans. They should have played Swansea again in May 1954, but the booking was cancelled due to Oliver Hardy's illness. On that occasion, they were replaced on the bill by Gladys Morgan, known as 'The Queen of Welsh Comedy'.

27 September

1898

Reports began to appear in a number of South African newspapers about the death of the well-known Swansea cyclist William Rosser. He had settled in the Transvaal, where he had married, and he and his wife had subsequently moved to Australia. However, news indicated that both of them had committed suicide by taking poison in Melbourne. His mother in Danygraig believed the reports, because it had been foretold in a dream in which she found herself 'in a huge pit resembling a grave. I had the same dream exactly some months ago just before I lost a daughter.'

1918

Chief Petty Officer George Prowse VC of the Royal Naval Reserve was killed in action. He was born in Llantrisant but worked as a collier at Grovesend Colliery and lodged at Station Road. He then married Sara Lewis from Treharne Road in Landore, where they lived before he was sent to France. Among a number of brave actions, Prowse led an assault on a German position on 2 September 1918, capturing twenty-three prisoners and five machine guns. He was consequently awarded the Victoria Cross. His luck ran out, however, later in the month when he led an attack on a machine-gun post and was killed by a single bullet near Arleux in France. The VC was awarded to his widow Sarah in July 1919. His grave has never been identified.

28 September

1825

The foundation stones of a new Town Hall and House of Correction were laid on this day by Richard Jeffreys, the portreeve. Detachments of the Swansea Cavalry led a procession from the old Town Hall to the site of the new. The portreeve deposited coins in a cavity and once a stone had been carefully lowered, he tapped it three times with a mallet. It was hoped that the Town Hall would be a 'habitation of judgement and justice'. The ceremony was repeated at the new House of Correction, which was intended to be 'a house of Mercy'.

1935

Swansea RFC defeated New Zealand 11–3 at St Helens. They thus became the first club team to beat an All Blacks side.

1969

On this day, Giorgio Chinaglia made his debut in Italian football's Serie A for Lazio against AC Milan. He became one of the highest-paid footballers of his generation, playing for Italy in the 1974 World Cup final and helping Lazio win the Serie A title. Chinaglia also enjoyed a highly successful career with the New York Cosmos football team and was named as the greatest player in Lazio's history during the club's centenary celebrations. Born in Italy, he was brought up in Cardiff and became an apprentice professional with Swansea Town. However, he was not regarded as good enough and was released by the club on a free transfer.

29 September

1801

'A man, intoxicated, got on the parapet wall of Swansea Castle, fell asleep, and, on waking, fell over into the yard of Mr Williams, ironmonger, a height of 60 feet, without receiving any other injury than a slight contusion on the head.' (*Bury and Norwich Post*)

1899

Uncle Robin announced a children's Map and Socks Competition in the *Cambrian News*. 'To the boy who sends in the best map of Carmarthenshire will be awarded a beautiful and valuable book, to the girl who sends in the best pair of knitted socks to suit a baby ... will be awarded a lovely work-basket.'

1982

It was reported in the *Evening Post* that a stuffed bear, which had for many years featured as an attraction in the Number 10 pub on Union Street, had been restored by a taxidermist. It had been damaged in January when it was dragged through the snow by vandals. 'Both ears, both front paws and a foot were cut off, some teeth were missing and the nose was non-existent. Part of the chest area had been slashed and removed.' Originally the bear had accompanied a German dance band on a visit to Swansea at the end of the nineteenth century. 'During the visit the bear died, but such was the affection in which it was held by the people of Swansea that it was stuffed and left behind.'

30 September

1864

John Thomas, a collier, was charged with smoking underground in a pit in Morriston, contrary to Special Rule 28. However, Mr Thomas was unaware that any such ban existed. He only spoke Welsh so could not understand instructions issued in English, and was illiterate, so could not understand the prominently displayed rules around the pit (he had also been given his own copy). He was accused of smoking in the most dangerous place in the colliery and risking the lives of twenty-five fellow workers. He was sent to prison for three months.

1898

The *Cambrian News* reported that Revd Harry Jones had returned to Swansea. He had attended Danygraig Board School, and worked as an assistant grocer at Landore and Morriston before emigrating to America in 1880 and joining the navy in 1896. He became chaplain on the US battleship *Texas* and during the Spanish-American War was known as 'the fighting parson'. He was injured in battle but 'in the fiercest of the conflict he was with the sailors, lending a hand whenever it was needed, and never flinching, though weak and ill enough to be in the hospital ... He exerted a moral influence over the men of his ship which will never be forgotten and was looked upon as a hero by the whole of the American Navy'. In October he appeared at the Temperance Hall in Swansea to give a talk, illustrated with 'lamplight views'.

2 October

1893

An advertisement showed a letter, allegedly written by F.J. Knight to the *South Wales Daily Post*, extolling the virtues of the 'Pontardawe Worm Lozenge', which he had bought for his 18-month-old daughter. She was wasting away and he feared for her life. However, after only one treatment she 'got rid of hundreds of thread worms'. By the time she had taken the contents of a $9^{1}/_{2}d$ box, she had expelled thousands. Her life had been saved by 'Pontardawe Worm Lozenges' from Mr Cliff, Chemist, of High Street Swansea.

1937

This was the date of the death of Swansea Jack – a dog and media star. He was a retriever who lived with his owner William Thomas on the Strand and made a habit of pulling people out of the dock. He is credited with saving twenty-seven humans (and two dogs) from drowning. His first rescue was a 12-year-old boy in 1931 but that went unreported. However, his fame grew as he allegedly rescued more people. The local council gave him a silver collar in thanks. In 1936 he was recognised as 'Bravest Dog of the Year'. In 2000, he was named 'Dog of the Century' by the Canine Defence League. Sadly the poor dog died as a result of eating rat poison. Some believe it was given to him deliberately.

3 October

1691

On this day, the Spanish vessel *El Dorado* was wrecked off Worms Head. According to local tradition, it was carrying gold and silver worth at least £80,000. This is the origin of the persistent stories of treasure washed up on to the shore at Rhosilli during storms. The wreck was apparently exposed in 1807 and 1833, when treasure was recovered before the incoming tide reclaimed it all for the sea.

1892

Henry Morton Stanley, journalist, explorer and politician, was granted the Freedom of Swansea in a ceremony at the Guildhall in recognition of his achievements. According to the *Cambrian News*, he delivered 'an important speech on the Dark Continent' and later, at a celebratory lunch at the Mackworth Hotel, he congratulated Swansea on becoming 'The Metallurgical Capital of the World'. He went on to express regret at the spread of education, which seemed 'to create rubbishy notions amongst the working classes'.

1904

The express train known as the *Flying Welshman*, which travelled from Milford to Paddington in eight hours, derailed as it approached Loughor Bridge. Two employees and three passengers were killed when two coaches toppled over. The injured were taken to Llanelli and Swansea, where onlookers rushed to the station to catch a glimpse of the victims.

4 October

1938

Miss Rees from Cwm School went to the Guildhall to be shown how to work out 'the size of mask (gas) suitable for each school child'. (Cwm School log)

1948

Sir Arthur Whitten-Brown was born in Glasgow in 1886. He served in the Royal Flying Corps and achieved fame on 15 June 1919 as navigator when he and John Alcock made the first non-stop transatlantic flight. It took them a little over sixteen hours, flying through fog so thick they couldn't see their propellers. At one point he stood up to clear frozen sleet from the plane behind him and at times they were forced to fly upside down. They were both knighted by King George V. In 1923 he became chief representative for the Metropolitan-Vickers Company in Swansea and worked as the manager of a light bulb factory from offices in Wind Street. He died on this day in his home at Belgrave Court in the Uplands from an accidental overdose of the sedative Veronal.

2006

Members of the Clydach Cavalry Full Gospel church set up a protest outside the Grand Theatre in Swansea to dissuade people from visiting a touring production called 'Puppetry of the Penis'. According to the billing, two (inevitably) 'well-endowed Australians' manipulated their manhood into 'various shapes, objects and landmarks'. The church members described the show as 'an abomination. It's abusing the body.' (*The Evening Post*)

9 October

1816

Fanny Imlay, the sister-in-law of the poet Percy Shelley, was found dead in the Mackworth Arms in Swansea. She had committed suicide by drinking a bottle of laudanum after arriving on a coach from Bristol. The reasons for her suicide probably lie in the tangled web of relationships within her family: some believe that she died because of her unrequited love for Shelley. She was buried in the churchyard of what is now St Matthew's church near High Street station. Shelley himself came to Swansea to arrange her funeral.

1857

The *Cambrian News* reported the creation of a fund for those who suffered in the Indian Rebellion. The meeting expressed sympathy with the victims, 'many of whom after enduring insult and outrage and scarce escaping with their lives, after seeing the dearest objects of their affection murdered before their eyes, are now in a state of destitution.' Donations began with £10 from the mayor and £25 from Mr Dillwyn, MP.

1940

Warning 7 p.m. All clear 8.50 p.m. We came home by bus. Arrived at Margaret Street – heavy AA firing commenced 9.20 p.m. No warning given. Incendiary bombs had been dropped one on garage (Waters) Margaret Street. No fire occurred bomb destroyed. Sheltered in house in Margaret Street home 9.45 p.m. Explosive bombs in some parts, incendiary bombs on hill.

(From an unnamed air-raid warden's diary held by West Glamorgan Archive Service)

13 October

1848

The body of a female infant was found buried in the sand on the beach at St Helens. The corpse was wrapped in brown paper, over which there was a piece of cloth. The baby weighed 7lbs and had been born alive, since the lungs had been inflated. The child had been dead for about eight days and there was a wound on the back of the head, which could have been caused if the mother had gone into labour unexpectedly. The mother was never traced. (*Cambrian News*)

1929

A BBC religious broadcast came from underground at The Chapel Down, Mynydd Newydd Pit in Fforestfach. It was one of the few collieries in the world where conditions were so bad that prayer meetings were held in an underground chapel before every shift.

1999

The BBC confirmed that American singer Diana Ross had flown into Swansea Airport in her private plane, a Cessna 560. She was met by a chauffeur-driven Mercedes and taken to film a special edition of *Top of the Pops* in Swansea. Diana Ross had first flown into the UK at Farnborough in order to avoid Heathrow, where she claimed she had previously been 'frisked' in an intrusive and over-enthusiastic manner.

16 October

1779

Margaret Mathews from Loughor was accused of poisoning her father, John Bevan. He was to marry his servant maid and as a wedding gift, he was planning to give her a piece of land. Margaret invited her father and potential stepmother over to supper, and made some 'milk and flour diet' using plenty of butter and sugar. John ate it and became violently ill. He 'retched and was purging blood most violently until 2.00 a.m. when he died,' convinced that the dinner was to blame. His stomach, when opened, was full of arsenic, but there was insufficient evidence to convict Margaret, 'the mother of three children and of unblemished character.' (*Oxford Journal*)

1929

Ivor Allchurch (1929–1997), 'the Golden Boy' of Swansea football, was born in Waun Wen. He left school at 14 to work as a fish market porter, but soon became an outstanding football player for Swansea and Wales. He appeared 445 times for Swansea, scoring 164 goals, later playing for Newcastle and Cardiff. Allchurch made 68 international appearances for Wales, scoring 23 goals, and he was awarded an MBE for services to football in 1966. A statue in his honour outside the Liberty Stadium was unveiled in 2005.

18 October

1674

Richard Nash (commonly known as Beau Nash), leader of fashionable society, was born in Swansea. He went to Jesus College, Oxford, and served briefly in the army and as a barrister, but it was as Master of Ceremonies in Bath that he achieved fame. It was an unofficial role but extremely influential. He would assess new arrivals for their suitability, arrange marriages, introduce dancing partners and regulate gambling. Nash died in 1761 and was buried in a pauper's grave. It is said that his mistress Juliana Popjoy, also known as Lady Betty Besom, was so distraught on his death that she moved to live in a large hollow tree near Warminster.

1961

Gladys Morgan appeared as a guest star in the *Good Old Days* television series from the stage of the City Varieties in Leeds. She was born in Swansea in 1898 and became known as the 'Queen of Comedy'. After early appearances in Swansea and Mumbles, she made a career in music hall with her husband Frank Laurie, who acted as her straight man. She was noted for her infectious laugh and expressive face. Morgan appeared in pantomime in Swansea as well as on radio and television, and eventually retired to Worthing, where there is a blue plaque in her honour. She died in 1983.

27 October

1838

The *Cambrian News* announced the death of John Langdon of St Vincent's Cottage, Swansea. He was 65 and had been a commander in the Royal Navy.

> This good and gallant officer fought and bled for his country. In the affair of the Dardanelles he lost his leg. On retiring into the quietude of domestic life, he practised the virtues of a sincere and pious Christian, a fond and affectionate Husband and parent. His loss will be most lamented by those who knew him best.

1914

Dylan Thomas was born at No. 5 Cwmdonkin Drive in the Uplands and spent his first thirty years in Swansea. His childhood is memorably documented in his writings. He left school in 1931 and worked as a journalist for the local paper, the *South Wales Daily Post*, for eighteen months while refining his poetry. He soon became highly regarded for his work. He always wished to be known as a poet but also achieved recognition as a serious drinker, an image he cultivated wth enthusiasm. He supplemented his income as best he could with reading tours and broadcasts, and wrote occasional scripts for the BBC and the Ministry of Information. Thomas was particularly popular in America and died of pneumonia during a reading tour in New York on 9 November 1953. His body was returned to Wales and buried in Laugharne.

28 October

1914

According to the head teacher's log book, playtime in Cwm School Bonymaen was suspended until 11.20 a.m. to enable the children to see the troops pass on the Great Western Railway on their way to the Front.

1933

On this day the decision was taken that the 'British Empire Panels' painted by Frank Brangwyn would be displayed in Swansea, in the new Assembly Hall in the Guildhall. They had originally been exhibited in Olympia but were deemed unsuitable for their intended location in the Royal Gallery in the Palace of Westminster; a new venue was required. They depict elements of the British Empire, though there is apparently no geographical logic behind them. They are entirely fantastical, illustrating a world of beauty and abundance. The architectural plans for the hall were adapted to accommodate them: the height of the Brangwyn Hall was raised to 13.4m to ensure their installation.

1940

The Borough Architect received a reply from the Minister of Home Security Camouflage Establishment concerning the camouflaging of the Guildhall. The ministry did not think it necessary 'so far as the national interest is concerned and would not make any grant if the council wished to proceed'. The idea was rejected due to the expense, and the architect added his own comment that 'it seems doubtful whether the building will be in any way effectively hidden'.

29 October

1897

The *Cambrian News* reported that Emily Rogers of Mumbles summoned her husband John for desertion. In defence, John argued that his wife led him an awful life, as she had a terrible temper. Sometimes when he was sitting by the fire, Emily would come suddenly behind him and would strike him on the head with a dishcloth. And once, when standing by the window, she pushed John down in a chair, and then pushed him and the chair out through the window. 'She has never washed my clothes yet,' John lamented. He was ordered to pay her 5s per week.

1940

Terence Hart, 19, a soldier from Swansea, was sentenced to one day's imprisonment at Bow Street Assizes in London. He and a colleague were detained whilst stealing from a West End tobacconist's shop that had been badly damaged during an air raid. They were both handed over to the military authorities. The previous night, they had 'rendered valuable assistance in rescuing injured persons from the debris of a damaged building'. (*Derby Daily Telegraph*)

1977

The Carlton Cinema in Oxford Street was closed by the Rank Organisation. It was eventually bought by Waterstones bookshop, which renovated the interior whilst preserving the front-of-house area.

9 November

1623

The Elizabethan historian and antiquarian William Camden died on this day in Chislehurst in 1623. In his influential work *Britannia* he noted that 'Swinesey is of great account, a towne so called by the Englishmen of Sea-Swine, but the Britains Aber-Taw, of the river Taw running by it.' The term 'sea swine' does not appear to have caught on, thankfully.

1888

It was reported that Frank Abbot and George Siddon of Swansea had applied for a patent for a method of advertising on seats and chairs. (*Cambrian News*)

1943

Future world heavyweight boxing champion Rocky Marciano arrived in Liverpool with the American 348th Combat Engineers and was immediately sent to Swansea to begin amphibious training. He remained in Mumbles for about a year. It is said that he once knocked a soldier through the window of Forte's ice cream parlour and was involved in an infamous brawl in the Adelphi pub in Swansea. As a result, he first began serious training at a gym run by Welsh heavyweight Jim Wilde in Rutland Street, where he began to learn how to channel his aggression. He took part in the D-Day landings and returned to America in November 1944, though some believe that he often returned to Swansea in disguise in later years to eat cockles and laverbread. (John Cameron, *Redemption*)

12 November

1900

The *Chicago Evening News* printed the story from Newfoundland of the sailor William Warwick from Swansea who, they claimed, had beaten 'all the world's records of fasting and endurance'. He had been stranded on a rock after leaving his ship *Little Pet* in search of provisions. He was there for twenty-seven days, suffering from gangrene, without food, proper clothing or shelter. When found he was 'reduced to a skeleton'. Warwick was taken to hospital where 'owing to the vermin embedded in his bones, the five toes of his right foot had to be amputated'.

1929

Following torrential rain, the level of Cray Reservoir on the road to Brecon had risen 5ft in one day. It was the highest recorded rainfall for almost thirty years. Swansea has always been acquainted with heavy rain and did not escape on this occasion, with Llansamlet being particularly badly affected. Residents believed that the raising of the level of the road had created a dam, which had retained water. Houses were inundated, livestock such as pigs and chickens were drowned and relief was taken to families along planks leading to their upstairs bedrooms. The *Evening Post* described the scene as a 'huge lake, rippling serenely in the morning sun'.

16 November

1888

The *Cambrian News* reported that two men were in Swansea, both of whom claimed to be Jack the Ripper. In one incident a drunken Swedish seaman called Olaf Olsen entered the house of Thomas Beynon on Howell Street and threatened him with a knife. When he announced that he was Jack the Ripper, Beynon chased him away with a poker. He was eventually caught by a group of men. Olsen was fined £1. At the same time another man entered the Mermaid public house and told the landlord that he was Jack the Ripper and was 'only having a look around before commencing operations'. He left the pub and disappeared. It was believed to be a hoax.

1907

Mary Ann Griffin, 22, was charged with the attempted murder of her husband, William. He had gone to work at Clyne Valley Colliery with a jug of tea and a treacle sandwich but was taken ill, as was the colleague with whom he shared it. On his return home Mary gave him some port and he lost consciousness. When he awoke he found himself tied to the bed with a strap around his neck and his hands bound. Neighbours found him in agony with the effects of carbolic acid poisoning. Mary pleaded guilty to attempted murder and apologised. She was sentenced to ten years' imprisonment. (*Weekly Mail*)

20 November

1802

The *Morning Post* carried the unfortunate story of a Mr Barrett from Neath, who had hoped to make an ascent in a hot air balloon. His purpose 'was frustrated by the intervention of his creditors from Swansea who took away the balloon from him but not without first breaking a lock and overpowering Mr B and his servant in a hard struggle. Poor Barrett had not a shilling where-with to bless himself. In his present distress by some he is condemned, pitied by many, compassionated but by a few.'

1942

Edgar Davies, a temporary constable in the Police War Reserve, appeared before a disciplinary enquiry in Swansea. He was accused first of being in the wrong place: he had been ordered to patrol the 'Vulnerable Point Beat' at the Morriston Gas Works, but had instead chosen to remain gossiping in the Aircraft Spotters' Post. Secondly, and more seriously, he was accused of being insubordinate 'by word and demeanour' to his superior, Acting Police Sergeant Harris. He was alleged to have said, 'Bach, you are one for discipline. Who are you to order me about? I will do as I please. You are like the Gestapo! Who do you think you are?' Davies was dismissed. (*Swansea Police War Reserve Disciplinary Report Book*)

23 November

1906

Under the headline 'Fish Frying Premises Gutted', the *Cambrian News* reported that the shop at No. 26 Wellington Street kept by Mrs Roberts was badly damaged in a fire. The cause of the fire was believed to be a stove that had overheated.

2001

A one-armed man was caught drink-driving after jumping a red light in his car while making a mobile phone call. The driver had lost his right arm below the elbow, and the police commented that 'he was not driving a car which had been adapted to accommodate his disability'. He was seen driving through a red traffic light holding a mobile phone to his ear with his good arm and subsequent tests showed that he had almost twice the legal limit of alcohol in his breath. He was given an eighteen-month driving ban, fined and ordered to pay costs totalling £450 by magistrates in Swansea.

2007

A woman from Clase was jailed for four months for receiving benefits after falsely claiming her husband had died. (She had previously claimed that he was her brother.) However, investigations showed they still lived together. It was discovered that she had received over £11,000 in council tax and housing benefit. The previous year the woman attempted to dodge a speeding fine by writing to a court in her daughter's name, claiming she was dead.

26 November

1842

A tradesman brought up his apprentice (before the police court), a lad of about 15 years, stating that he was a most incorrigible 'mitcher'. The boy said he did not like his trade. He was severely reprimanded and warned, with an assurance that if he offended in a similar manner again he would be committed to the House of Correction.

(Cambrian News)

1946

Mr Tanner of St Thomas, a Swansea Council employee, spoke to a Norwegian colleague named T. Danielson in the electrical department about his wartime experiences serving on submarine HMS *Seawolf*. During an attack, it had torpedoed a German steamer off the Norwegian town of Mendal. This was Danielson's hometown and he revealed that his father had been out shooting birds in the fjord when the attack happened. The steamer was carrying a large cargo of tinned meat for German troops, which fell into the sea in crates. Danielson recovered 1,600kg of meat, which was distributed to the local people who lived throughout the winter on a dish which became known as 'Torpedo hash'. (*The Evening Post*)

2003

The Palace Theatre in Swansea was sold at auction for £340,000 in an auction at BAFTA in London. It was one of only two purpose-built music halls in the UK and was also the first place in Wales to screen a moving picture.

28 November

1760

After touring along the Bristol Channel collecting recruits for the Royal Navy using a press gang, the *Caesar* left Swansea for Plymouth. There were at least sixty-eight 'recruits' chained in the hold. However, the tide and the weather were against them and they turned back. Tragically the ship became disorientated in heavy weather and mistook Pwlldu Head for Mumbles. The *Caesar* crashed into the rocks and the side of the ship was ripped open. The officers and some members of the crew managed to scramble ashore and made their way to Pennard, but their cargo were all drowned. The captain, Adam Drake, said that sixty-five men and three women had been lost. The villagers of Pennard, however, claimed to have found ninety-three bodies, which were buried in a mass grave on Pwlldu, called Gravesend. It is still marked by a circle of stones in the bracken.

1929

There was a devastating explosion during the afternoon shift at the Wernbwll Colliery at Penclawdd, and seven bodies were recovered. An inquest could not determine the cause of the explosion and the pit remained open until September 1937. During the last shift, miner Sid James was killed by a roof fall.

30 November

1833

Evan Sims, aged 15, died suddenly at the Hope and Anchor public house 'while in the act of dancing'. The *Cambrian News* goes on: 'It appeared that the deceased had not been in the house many minutes and was perfectly sober. Verdict: died by the visitation of God.'

1839

The *Cambrian News* reported a 'deaf and infirm old man, named Richards' was crossing High Street when he was knocked down by a coach horse, 'and before the coachman was aware of the circumstance, the wheels had passed over his body, which caused his death shortly after'. One of the passengers inside the coach, Mr Watson from Llanelly, wrote a letter to the paper:

> I do acquit the driver of all blame. He is a respectable man, very careful, and was not driving at an improper rate. No one could have expected that the deceased would have so heedlessly placed himself in contact with the leaders. It has been said the unfortunate man was 72 years of age, dull of hearing, and near sighted. If so, had he no relatives or friends that he was so exposed at midnight?

1916

The *Cambrian Daily Leader* carried the following advertisement: 'Penhale's Mourning Department. Ladies costumes and gentlemen's suits, black serge or vicuna, from 50s. All goods made on premises. Orders executed in eight hours where necessary.'

5 December

1736

Thomas Morgan of Llansamlet was charged with breaking and entering the house of Thomas Popkin and stealing two forks. He was found guilty and transported for seven years.

1916

The *Cambrian News* featured the following article:

> Stone throwing nuisance. Three boys were charged with throwing stones to the danger of the public. The Chief Constable had received a complaint about the boys, who had since received a good 'lamming' 'from their parents. The parents were ordered to pay a fine of 5s each.

1950

A fine of £150 was imposed on David Lloyd, a draper of Penfilia Road, by the judge at Swansea Assizes for refusing to answer a summons to appear on a jury. When he had failed to turn up in November, a police detective constable had tried to serve a summons on him, but he refused. The following day Inspector Dunford left one on the counter of his shop, but Lloyd threw it into the street, saying: 'I am not accepting it. I do not want anything to do with the law. I deal with a higher authority.' (*Dundee Courier*)

6 December

1828

Mr Powell, the House Surgeon of the Swansea Infirmary, reported a large number of new smallpox cases. He regretted the reluctance of some parents to bring their children for vaccination – which was still regarded with suspicion, particularly 'among the lowest class in whose dirty and ill-ventilated houses disease is more likely to prove destructive.' (*Cambrian News*)

1878

At Bonymaen, Catherine Hopkins, the widow of Hopkin Hopkins, died aged 100, 'deeply lamented by a large circle of friends'. (*Cambrian News*)

1919

The *South Wales Weekly Post* reported that the Glamorgan Education Committee had decided to dismiss sixteen married female teachers, giving them three months' notice. They were aware of 'several cases of married couples, both husband and wife being teachers in the employ of the committee, drawing salaries that together amounted to various sums ranging between £548 and £755 per annum. In due course both husband and wife would be entitled to pensions. Was it right that both husband and wife should draw a pension from the State?' A committee member declared that when a woman married, her duty was to look after the home, and the Director of Education added that married women teachers became head mistresses and so blocked promotion for men.

9 December

1832

Eleanor Williams was found dead in a well at Felindre, having been beaten. No one was ever tried for her murder, though local opinion accused Robert Thomas of Llywngwenno Farm, where she worked as a servant for his father. Robert was also rumoured to be the father of her unborn child. For many years afterwards, on the anniversary of her death, her memorial gravestone was painted red by local people. In 1849, Robert Thomas was fined for damaging the tombstone with a hatchet.

1950

Phillip Llewellyn, a 26-year-old labourer, was so ashamed of his clothes that he stole those of another lodger in the house where he was staying in Swansea. He took a shirt, a pullover, a pair of socks and a tie from Daniel O'Sullivan, with whom he shared a room. When he was detained by the police, he had all the items in his possession, apart from the tie. Llewellyn claimed that he needed the clothes in order to visit his dying father in Swansea hospital and could not afford to buy any. He was told in court that 'there is no excuse for a young able-bodied man not having any money these days', and was sentenced to three months' imprisonment. (*Gloucester Citizen*)

13 December

1806

A thunderbolt struck a field in Birchgrove, killing two horses and two sheep, without inflicting 'any apparent injury to either'. The farmer recalled that no noise beyond that of the thunder was noticed at the time. (*Cambrian News*)

1935

Amy Dillwyn was born in Sketty in 1845 and died on 13 December 1935. She inherited the Dillwyn Spelter Works in Llansamlet from her father in 1892 and became a pioneering female industrialist. She was able to transform the fortunes of an ailing business and preserve jobs for the workers. Amy was a social reformer who campaigned for female suffrage and was well known in Swansea for her unorthodox lifestyle, referring to her friend Olive Talbot as her 'wife'. Amy was also a highly regarded novelist; she wrote six novels including *The Rebecca Rioter*. Her house, Ty Glyn, is now Mumbles Nursing Home.

1995

The mummy of Tem Hor, held in Swansea Museum, was given an X-ray at the Royal Gwent Hospital in Newport. It showed that there was a slight fracture to a rib, but that this was not the cause of death, which appears to have happened from natural causes.

19 December

1845

The *Cambrian News* used the headline 'Juvenile Depravity' to describe 15-year-old Rachel Morris, who was charged with stealing 4s 9d from the house of Captain Bowden, where she had been babysitting. She took money from a drawer to buy 'white muslin dresses, with velvet bodies, artificials, etc for the purpose of attending one of the two-penny Christmas balls – the hotbeds for the production and growth of young delinquents to be held in High Street. These fine dresses were found in a house in Mount-Pleasant where rooms were let to young girls, for the purpose of getting up the dresses without the knowledge of their parents.' Rachel had, however, spent some of the money on the purchase a bottle of rum. Captain Bowden agreed not to prosecute and she was released into the care of her parents.

1972

One of the most important groups in the history of Welsh rock music was 'Man'. Their Christmas concert at the Patti Pavilion on this date acquired legendary status and the live recording has a significant cult following.

2013

The BBC website reported that the Swansea coastguards had taken a distress call from three people in a capsized dingy at 07.15 GMT. However, the incident was actually taking place off the coast of Swansea, New South Wales, in Lake Macquarie. The call was rerouted to Australian coastguards, who carried out a successful rescue.

26 December

1838

The death of Ann Hatton (1764–1838) was announced. She wrote popular novels under the pseudonym 'Ann of Swansea'. As a child she was scarred by smallpox and lost an eye after being accidentally shot whilst working in a London brothel. She went on to spend time in America, where she wrote the first known libretto by a woman to the opera *Tammany: The Indian Chief*. She then settled in Swansea in 1799, where she ran a bathing house and later a dancing school in Kidwelly. Her novels included the controversial *Chronicles of an Illustrious House* (1816), a satire on Swansea set in the town of 'Gooselake'. In her old age she received an allowance from her family on the condition that she lived a minimum of 100 miles away from their home in London.

1948

The pantomime at the Swansea Empire Theatre on Lower Oxford Street began its twice-daily seasonal performances. The production was *Goody Two Shoes*, the story of a magical pair of shoes given to Goody as a reward for goodness but which were substituted for a naughty pair by a wicked dwarf. Low down on the bill were Morecambe and Wise, playing the characters of Late and Early. Their partnership had begun after a chance meeting in Swansea a few years previously.

1931

John Charles (1931–2004) was born in Cwmbwrla and achieved great acclaim as an outstanding footballer for Leeds United and Juventus in Italy. He had originally been on the ground staff at Swansea Town but never played for the first team. Charles joined Leeds United in 1948 and became a central figure in the club, playing initially at centre half and then at centre forward. In the 1956/57 season, he scored 38 goals in 40 appearances in the First Division. At the end of the season, Charles was signed to Juventus for a record transfer fee of £65,000, and he was so successful that in his first season he was voted as the best player in Italy. He was a much-loved figure at the club: in 1997 the fans voted him the best foreign player ever to have played for Juventus.

Charles played for Wales 38 times and scored 15 goals. He was awarded the CBE in 2001 and granted the freedom of the city of Swansea in 2003. In that same year, the Football Association of Wales recognised him as the outstanding Welsh player of the previous fifty years.

1976

The legendary South Wales comedian Ryan Davies started his fifth consecutive season in pantomime in Swansea Grand Theatre. On this occasion he appeared in *Babes in the Wood*. He died on holiday in New York after completing the season.

29 December

1804

The London Mail of Friday last did not arrive here till near eleven o'clock that night, having been delayed seventeen hours at the Passage House on the other side of the Severn, in consequence of large shoals of ice floating down the river, which rendered it unsafe for the Mail Boat to cross till Friday morning.

(*Cambrian News*)

1974

William Fuller, born in Laugharne in 1884, was sent as a child to the Swansea Industrial School for truants in Bonymaen. He found his vocation when he joined the Welsh Regiment, serving initially in the Boer War. During the First World War, he was promoted to lance corporal and in September 1914 was fighting at the Battle of the Aisne. He ran into heavy German fire in order to recover his wounded colleague, Captain Mark Haggard (nephew of the novelist Rider Haggard). Fuller carried him for about 100 yards back to cover before returning to rescue his rifle. Sadly Haggard died of his wounds but the rescue fired the popular imagination and Fuller was awarded the Victoria Cross. Later, in June 1938, Fuller rescued two boys stranded on a sandbank in Swansea Bay by the incoming tide. He died at his home at No. 55 Westbury Street, Swansea, on this day in 1974. He is buried at Oystermouth.

30 December

1898

If the choice were given to most people whether to accept good wishes for a Happy Christmas, or for a Happy New Year, the popular vote would be for the latter. The Happy Christmas belongs to youths, most middle-aged folk having abandoned such hopes … Jollity seems to have departed, and a sober, very material character taken its place. The average Briton desires to be quietly happy, and above all to be comfortable.

(The Ladies' Column, *Cambrian News*)

1942

A vital part of the preparations for the invasion of Europe in the Second World War was underway in Swansea on this day. This was PLUTO – the Pipeline Under the Ocean. This was a means of delivering essential petrol quickly to the Continent in order to resupply motorised transport and weapons and maintain the advance. Approximately 27 miles of 2in pipe, capable of delivering 125 tons or 38,000 gallons a day, were laid under the Bristol Channel by HMS *Holdfast*, linking Queens Dock in Swansea and Watermouth Bay in Ilfracombe. The system underwent long-term trials starting in December 1942, which were extremely successful. Once the invasion had taken place, the system delivered fuel very efficiently to Boulogne. The recovery of the extensive pipeline was a huge salvage operation lasting two years, during which 800 miles of the 1,000-mile-long project was recovered.

Lightning Source UK Ltd.
Milton Keynes UK
UKOW07f1143040215

245676UK00003B/3/P